The
Cultural
Personality

D. Paul Schafer

Rock's Mills Press
Oakville, Ontario
2018

Published by
ROCK'S MILLS PRESS
Published by arrangement with the author. All rights reserved.

Contents

Preface

Profound changes are taking place in the cultural complexion of the world. Not only is the world in a state of dynamic and rapid change, but a whole new era is also opening up in community, regional, national, and international affairs.

Situated squarely in the middle of these developments are people as individuals, as well as members of groups and citizens of countries. With all the changes going on in the world in economic systems, political practices, technological processes, religious beliefs, environmental policies, and demographic patterns, now is a propitious time to be enquiring into the roles and responsibilities of people as individuals in the world.

What is most apparent about this is how difficult it is for most people to cope with all the changes and developments going on in the world. This is largely because the two basic personality types that have driven world history and human behavior over the last two centuries—the economic personality and the specialist personality—are breaking down.

The concept of the economic personality is breaking down because it treats people as producers and consumers of goods, services, and material wealth at a time when these practices are having a devastating effect on the natural environment and, as well, not bringing people the satisfaction and happiness they expected to find in them. The idea of the specialist personality is breaking down because it encourages people to develop only a single skill and occupation when change is occurring so rapidly throughout the world that people's areas of specialization are often out-of-date not long after they were acquired as a result of extraordinary de-

velopments in technology, communications, artificial intelligence, robotics, and a great deal else.

As a result of these developments, and others, people in all parts of the world are having the utmost difficulty coping with the problems of the present and prospects for the future. Clearly a new prototype of the human personality is needed to come to grips with these problems and prospects, as well as to drive human behavior and produce more fulfillment, meaning, and contentment in life and in the world.

Many people are turning to religion or returning to religion in the hope of finding solutions to these problems and developing this new type of personality. Virtually all the religions in the world—Christianity, Hinduism, Islam, Judaism, Buddhism, and so forth—contend that people will be able to confront the present and deal more effectively with the future by becoming deeply immersed in religion, making a strong commitment to the values, teachings, and beliefs of the faith, and adhering to these values, teachings, and beliefs as fully as possible.

Others have a different approach. They are searching for this new personality type by engaging in meditation or yoga, living in the present rather than the future or the past, and experiencing higher levels of consciousness through the teachings of scholars such as Eckhart Tolle, Deepak Chopra, Wayne Dyer, and others. Countless people are also turning to mystics, evangelists, and other spiritual leaders who possess powerful beliefs and convictions about how these capabilities and this personality can be realized in fact.

To date, little consideration has been given to culture and the role it can play in dealing with these problems and producing this new personality type. And yet, culture possesses a remarkable potential to achieve this, largely by creating the cultural personality to come to grips with the problems of the present and the challenges and limitless possibilities of the future.

If most people were asked today what they thought the term "the cultural personality" means, they would probably say it describes a person who is actively involved in the arts, humanities, and finer things of life or has a great deal of knowledge and understanding of these matters. This is because this is what it meant to be a "cultured person" in the past and what it continues to mean for many people.

While this is a very essential aspect of the cultural personality, it ignores many of the larger and more fundamental dimensions of this specific personality type that are relevant at present and bound to be much more relevant in the future. Indeed, when all the various ways culture manifests in the world are examined and considered in totality—from the narrower artistic, humanistic, and historical ones to the broader psychological, anthropological, ecological, and cosmological ones—they produce an understanding of the cultural personality as a person who is able to live a full and fulfilling cultural life and to live life as an "ordered whole" in the fullest and most complete, compelling, and all-encompassing sense. To do this is to place people in the strongest possible position to deal with the difficult and demanding problems of the present as well as the limitless challenges and opportunities of the future in all areas of life, from the most mundane and commonplace to the most ideal and sublime.

It would be foolhardy to contend that it is possible to deal with the immensity, complexity, and profundity of the cultural personality in this book. What the book attempts to do is provide a comprehensive framework for coming to grips with many of the most salient aspects and characteristics of this particular personality type. It does so by postulating an "ideal prototype of the cultural personality" against which people can measure the reality of their own experience and to which they can look for guidance in times of adversity. It is a prototype based on the belief that culture in general and the cultural personality in particular provide the most effective avenues and means for dealing with the present and the future in all areas of life.

This book is divided into five chapters. In Chapter One, an assessment is made of the context within which people find themselves in the world today. In Chapter Two, the cultural personality is examined as a concept, largely by juxtaposing the two interdependent concepts of "culture" and "personality." In Chapter Three, the main characteristics of the cultural personality are revealed. In Chapter Four, the cultivation of the qualities and abilities that are most required to constitute the cultural personality are provided. And in Chapter Five, attention is given to the way the cultural personality can function most effectively in the world in practical terms.

Over the course of my life, I have had the good fortune to work closely with many people in different parts of the world who epitomize the cultural personality in certain ways. I would like to thank these people wholeheartedly for all the help, guidance, and advice they have given me over the years. They are all people who are or were deeply immersed in culture and specific aspects of culture in their own right, and made culture the centerpiece of their lives in one form or another.

The following people are included in this group: Jack Fobes, Guy Métraux, Prem Kirpal, Mochtar Lubis, Eleonora Barbieri Masini, Magda Cordelle McHale, Erika Erdmann, Paul Braisted, Robert Vachon, Biserka Cvjetičanin, Gao Xian, Herman Greene, Diane Dodd, George Simons, Grant Hall, Ashfaq Ishaq, Máté Kovacs, Manickam Nadarajah, Ronald Lessem, Thierry Dufay, Engelbert Ruoss, Alexander Schieffer, Teresa Torres Eca, Tony Duke, Brian Holihan, Jaber AlQallaf, Sheila Jans, Walter Pitman, André Fortier, John Hobday, Tom Symons, Joyce Zemans, James Gillies, Mavor Moore, Peter Mousaferiadis, Leslie Oliver, Joy MacFayden, Doug Worts, Bill Thachuk, Frank Pasquill, Peter Sever, John Gordon, Vincent Tovell, Gilles Lefebvre, John Meisel, and Donald Chen.

I would like to pay a special tribute to Galyna Shevchenko, Director of the Scientific Research Institute of the Spiritual Development of Man and International UNESCO Chair in Spiritual and Cultural Values of Upbringing and Education at Volodymyr Dahl East Ukrainian National University for the valuable role she has played in the development of my research and writing on culture in general and the cultural personality in particular. Not only has she been a great source of inspiration and motivation in this regard, but also she arranged to have an earlier version of *The Cultural Personality* I wrote for the World Culture Project in 1991 translated into Russian and published in Kyiv in 2017. Her dedicated work in this area of culture over many years has contributed substantially to making the concept of the cultural personality a subject of growing interest and popularity.

Finally, I would like to thank my family—my wife Nancy and daughters Charlene and Susan—for the valuable contributions they have made to my work on culture in all its diverse forms and manifestations. I would also like to thank David Stover, my publisher and good friend, for the indispensable role he has played in publishing many of my books on culture and Canadian culture and now this book on *The Cultural Personality*. I am very grateful to him for this, since these efforts have been such an integral part of my life in so many different ways.

D. Paul Schafer
Markham, Canada
2018

Live in the whole, in the good, in the beautiful.
JOHANN WOLFGANG VON GOETHE

Follow your bliss and the universe will open
doors where there are only walls.
JOSEPH CAMPBELL

Chapter One
The Context of the Cultural Personality

The study of culture properly begins with the study of the cultural elements of the individual.

—James Feibleman,
The Theory of Human Culture[1]

Culture and Personality. Personality and Culture. Profound words. Evocative words. Separately, these words conjure up very different images. Together, they combine to form the cultural personality, one of the most relevant and timely concepts of the human personality to appear on the global horizon in a very long time.

In an historical sense, there could be no more auspicious time to be enquiring into the nature of the cultural personality. With all the economic, environmental, social, political, and technological changes taking place in the world, could there be a better time than the present to be enquiring into the character, roles, responsibilities, and cultivation of people with respect to the development of their personalities and their lives?

From all accounts, more and more people in the world are having the utmost difficulty coping with the trials and tribulations of the modern world and prospects for the future. Why is this? What vortex of forces is at work throughout the world that is making it difficult for people to confront the present and future with hope,

1. James Feibleman, *The Theory of Human Culture* (New York: Humanities Press, 1968), p. 5.

optimism, and enthusiasm rather than pessimism, anxiety, and apprehension?

It is not difficult to identify the main forces. Since many of these forces are external in nature, they will be examined first. Following this, it will be possible to examine many of the forces that are internal in nature.

First of all, there are all the myriad changes taking place in contemporary economic systems. So pronounced and complex are the changes that are occurring in production and distribution methods, job and income practices, taxation policies, capital and labour arrangements, and employment possibilities that people in all parts of the world are having a great deal of difficulty coping with them. It is not only the complexity of these changes which is causing problems for most people, it is also the size, rapidity, and pervasiveness of these changes. In today's world, it is difficult for people to deal with increases in the cost of living, decreases in the standard of living, the emergence of larger and larger trading blocks and economic superstates, the concentration of income, wealth, and power in fewer and fewer hands, escalations in public and private debts, and the operations of multinational corporations. All these developments, and others, are producing a sense of uneasiness that people will be less and less able to earn a living and come to grips with the difficulties they are experiencing in a world that is in perpetual motion.

Such concerns are by no means limited to people living in particular parts of the world or working in specific occupations. On the contrary, they are shared by the vast majority of people in Africa, Asia, Latin America, North America, Europe, and the Middle East, as well as people working in every conceivable profession. With all the profound changes that are taking place in the ownership of business and industry, the nature of jobs, more and more contract, seasonal, and part-time work, labour-management relations, higher and higher prices for consumer goods, services, and accommodation, and the location of economic activities, who is not seriously concerned about their future economic situation, as well as the ability to make ends meet?

If economic changes are proving difficult to cope with, so are technological changes. It is not only the transformations going on in the nature of employment as well as the character of the marketplace that are proving difficult to deal with. It is also the fact that technology is transforming virtually every aspect of private and public life.

Clearly technology is a double-edged sword. On the one hand, it opens up countless opportunities for the storage, retrieval, and utilization of knowledge, information, and ideas, thereby making it possible *in principle* for people everywhere in the world to enjoy the benefits that are derived from learning, discovery, and access to the tangible and intangible cultural heritage of humankind. On the other hand, it makes it difficult *in practice* to adjust to the demands and dictates of a computer-oriented, media-dependent, and digital-dominated world.

While the cruelties of war, famine, poverty, human rights abuses, and corruption are never easy to deal with, prior to the computer and digital revolutions people had sufficient time to absorb such changes as the invention of the printing press, the telephone, radio, and television because images and information moved around the world much more slowly than they do today. Now, all that has changed. When news about racial violence, starvation, genocide, wars, military coups, tornadoes, earthquakes, and natural catastrophes can be transmitted to every nook and cranny of the world the instant they are happening, it takes an enormous amount of psychological endurance and intellectual fortitude on the part of people everywhere in the world to cope with this. It is one thing to learn about the devastation of a hurricane, flood, or war in another part of the world in a newspaper, magazine, or book sometime after they happened; it is quite another to see them unfolding before your very eyes.

If it is difficult to adjust to media assaults and digital attacks on people's senses that are going on every minute of every day, it is even more difficult to accept the prediction that there will be more and faster technological change in the future. Rather than being able to look forward to a period of relative calm, tranquility, and a slowing down of technological growth, all the evidence points in the opposite direction, namely to a speeding up of technological change in the years and decades ahead. With increased expenditure on computers, computer systems, satellite communications, telecommunications, many different types of phones, robotics, artificial intelligence, and so forth, it could scarcely be otherwise. Without doubt, it will take a great deal of fortitude on the part of all people in the world to make the transition to living when every day feels like the industrial revolution.

If economic and technological change is proving difficult to deal with, so is political change. Not only are many countries undergoing fundamental transformations in their political ideologies and constitutional arrangements, but also they are experiencing numerous transformations in governmental procedures and bureaucratic practices. It is hard to think of a country anywhere in the world today that is not being forced to contend with basic changes in democratic or socialist institutions, conservative or liberal ideologies, demands for independence and sovereignty, and shifts in political and governmental power. Whereas the political arena was once rather stable, as recent events in the United States, Great Britain, continental Europe, Africa, Asia, Latin America, Canada, and the Middle East have demonstrated in recent years, it is now very dynamic.

Countless developments on the ecological and environmental front are compounding the rate, complexity, and pervasiveness of these economic and political changes. Whereas the environment was taken for granted only three or four decades ago, presumably because of the belief that technology will eventually conquer nature and control the natural world, today a whole new type of environmental consciousness is sweeping the globe. Rather than controlling the environment as was commonly assumed, technology has been running roughshod over the natural environment. As this happens, a whole new set of environmental policies and practices come into play, except in certain countries such as the United States that are resisting these policies and practices at the present time. While it will take decades to undo the damage caused by unfettered technological change and rapid and excessive economic growth, the exponential consumption of renewable and non-renewable resources, colossal amounts of atmospheric pollution, rising levels of pollution, and mountains of industrial and human waste, it is undeniable that a new environmental consciousness is imperative if the globe's fragile ecosystems are to be preserved and protected in the years and decades ahead.

This new environmental awareness is mandatory in

a world threatened by continuous population growth in absolute terms. Even the most optimistic forecasts indicate that expanding numbers, especially when they are etched against shrinkages in arable land and depletion of the world's non-renewable resources, may be one of the most difficult, demanding, and debilitating problems of all. While urbanization may offer a temporary reprieve in a purely physical sense, largely by sanctioning vertical as opposed to horizontal development and compressing more and more people into the same space, it does so at an exorbitant price. Not only does it dramatically increase the amount of air, water, noise, and traffic pollution, but also it makes it difficult to maintain the level of social, recreational, and human amenities that are necessary for a healthy and sustained existence.

Finally, there are all the social and demographic changes going on in the world. Not only are societies becoming increasingly pluralistic in character, thereby increasing the potential for racism, racial conflict, and ethnic unrest, but also there is the revolution going on in the social media, relations between the sexes, and the aging population in most parts in the world. Whereas the former changes are having a profound effect on relationships between people within and between countries as well as on immigration and emigration rates and population movements, the latter changes are transforming the whole spectrum of relations between men and women as well as between younger and older generations. Relations in these areas, which were once rather well-defined and somewhat stable, are now up in the air and very dynamic. Moreover, it is impossible to predict where they will go in the future.

When all these economic, technological, political, environmental, social, and demographic changes are placed side by side and added up, they produce the portrait of a world that is in a state of revolutionary if not cataclysmic change. Under these circumstances, it is easy to see why more and more people everywhere in the world are feeling confused, frightened, disoriented, and insecure. It is not that all of these changes are negative. In fact, many of them, like the quest for equality between the sexes, longer lives, and environmental conservation, are exceedingly positive. It is just that they are compounding at such a rapid rate, and are so gargantuan in their size and significance, that they are making it difficult for people to come to grips with them. While there may be a grain of truth in the old adage that "the more things change, the more they stay the same," this would seem to be anything but the case today. In fact, in the modern world, change itself is the problem. Its rapidity, complexity, and propinquity have become so prominent and pronounced that people everywhere in the world are finding it exceedingly difficult to cope with it.

Regrettably, many of the traditional safeguards and support mechanisms that have been designed to counteract or deal with these problems are also undergoing profound transformations. This is tending to heighten and highlight the sense of anxiety and apprehension that many people are feeling.

At the elementary level, there are all the escape mechanisms and recreational outlets that people have evolved over the centuries to provide a counterpoise to excessive or revolutionary change. Whereas it was once possible to escape from the relentlessness of societal and global change through access to nature, walks in the countryside, long weekends, holidays, and travel, fewer and fewer people are able to take advantage of these opportunities for rest, relaxation, and recuperation. The reasons for this are not difficult to detect. Either modern economic, technological, political, and social systems are compelling people to be part of these systems all the time, or people lack the financial resources and leisure time to take advantage of these opportunities. In either case, it is less and less possible for people in all parts of the world to engage in those therapeutic measures and recuperative possibilities that are necessary to enable the mind, body, soul, and spirit to recover from the demands and dictates of a hectic and speeded-up existence.

To compound this problem, at the more profound level, there is the breakdown in many of the traditional social systems and support structures that have been developed over the centuries to deal with the consequences of dynamic and relentless change. While it was once possible to look to the family, the neighbourhood, or the community to cushion the shocks of profound economic, social, technological, political, demographic, and environmental dislocations, today this no longer seems possible. In an age where the family, kinship relationships, neighbourhoods, and communities are in a considerable state of flux, if not breaking down entirely, individuals are finding it more and more difficult to turn to these conventional sources of stability and relief to counteract the stresses and strains of modern life. While many new social systems and support structures are in the process of formation, particularly among women, the elderly, young people, and the disadvantaged, they are in such an embryonic state of development at the present time that it is highly unlikely that they will provide the stability, security, and order that is needed for a long time.

Concomitant with these developments is the erosion that has been taking place in traditions, roots, and identities. In the past, if transformations at the local, regional, national, or international level were proving difficult to cope with and there were not a lot of safety nets and support structures in place to provide help, it was always possible to look to traditions, roots, and identities for consolation, guidance, and solidarity. Even here, however, it is harder and harder to find solace, stability, security, and relief. Either these traditional touchstones are undergoing dramatic transformations of their own, or they are being rapidly eroded along with everything else. One need only look at the impact of the social media on Africa, Asia, Latin America, North America, Europe, or the Middle East to realize how difficult it is to maintain individual and collective identities in a world characterized by relentless and pervasive change.

At the most profound level of all, these problems are being severely tested and aggravated by the slow and steady erosion in moral values, ethical beliefs, and spiritual practices in many parts of the world. While the erosion of these venerable ideals and convictions has been going on for some time, it has been particularly rapid in the latter part of the past century and early part of the present century. Not only has there been a challenging of ethical, moral, religious, and spiritual authority in many parts of the world, but also there has been a steadily evolving sense of skepticism over the ability of the world's religions and religious institutions to provide effective answers to a whole host of contemporary problems. Even in parts of the world where there have been concerted attempts to adhere to or bring about religious revivals, such as in the Middle East with Islamic fundamentalism or in Europe and North America with new

Christian movements, it is apparent that these attempts are driven far more by a desire to return to the past than by an ability to confront the present and the future.

What seems to be lurking behind all these contemporary developments is a growing realization that a matrix of problems has emerged throughout the world that stands well beyond the theoretical systems and practical structures that have been designed to deal with them. Whether it is world population growth, the immigration and refugee crisis, poverty, environmental degradation, growing inequalities in income and wealth, the breakdown of social mores and institutions, or the erosion of moral, ethical, religious, and spiritual values, there is a sinking feeling in many parts of the world that the present global system may be on the verge of collapse. It is not only political ideologies, economic theories, social conventions, and religious practices that are being severely tested. More fundamentally, it is the whole legacy of accumulated knowledge, wisdom, and understanding that is being shaken to its very foundations.

The combined effect of these developments is that more and more people are feeling powerless to deal with these changes. Whereas it was once possible to look outside the self for help in coping with the consequences of dynamic and revolutionary change, this is far less possible. In today's world, perhaps more than any other day before it, people are being thrust back on their own resources and forced to confront the fallout from all these developments and changes without the benefit of external sources of support or reliable safety nets. This is coming at a time when profound transformations are taking place in the psychological make-up and well-being of people. But how could it be otherwise? With all the revolutionary changes that are going on in the external world of reality, is it any wonder that revolutionary changes are also going on in the internal world of the self?

For one thing, the whole notion of the individual as a one-dimensional person that has dominated the world for so long is no longer viable. Not only has specialization made it difficult for people to relate to one another, but also it has produced people who are fragmented, compartmentalized, and incomplete. Under these circumstances, is it any wonder that more and more people are finding it difficult to fuse body, mind, emotions, soul, spirit, and senses together in a meaningful and symbiotic relationship?

To complicate the matter, much of the psychological literature that has been designed to help people cope with their innermost fears and frustrations and most fundamental problems and difficulties seems to confound rather than simplify this situation. Whether it is the writings of psychologists such as Freud, Jung, Adler, Maslow, Laing, or others, much of this literature seems to raise more questions about human nature and behaviour than it answers at present. While in the long-run this may prove enormously helpful and a necessary state of affairs, at present it is of little consolation in helping people to confront the complex psychological problems that are being produced in a world that is in the throes of profound transformational change. It is as if people were bobbing up and down on the sea of life without a paddle or rudder. So much time and energy are spent trying to cope with the system and stay afloat that little or no time is left over to get one's bearings and chart one's future course.

While the desire to solve these problems is stronger than ever, the lack of understanding as to how this can be accomplished is producing a state of paralysis and uncertainty in the world that is as endemic as it is pervasive. People's actions have become so insignificant and inconsequential in the larger scheme of things that their sense of anxiety and apprehension is tinged with a kind of resignation and despair.

Under these circumstances, it is imperative to ask where we commence the search for potential solutions to these problems.

It is natural to turn first to the real world to see if there are any role models here after which people can pattern their own behaviour. After all, the ability to seek out and imitate or emulate role models has always been a potent source of human action and inspiration. Regrettably, however, there seems to be very few role models in the modern world capable of performing this function.

When professional classes and visible elites manifest greater concern with power, prestige, money, profits, and people's votes than with justice, equality, jobs, and the needs and rights of others, it is apparent that such groups do not provide viable role models on which people can predicate their behaviour in the future. Moreover, many of the individuals, institutions, and groups that do provide valuable role models in this respect lack the media attention, social status, and public recognition and attention that are required to have an impact on human conduct. Nevertheless, even if they were able to supply the moral and ethical leadership that is required, they are having their own problems coping with the complexities of a computer-powered, media-driven, and problem-infected world.

If it is not possible to find the clues that are necessary in role models that exist in the modern world, the next place to look is at personality prototypes after which people can pattern their own behavior and personal actions and aspirations.

While many such personality prototypes exist, two in particular stand heads and shoulders above the rest in today's world as indicated earlier, since they are so fundamentally connected to contemporary life and consequently to the object of our investigation. The first is "the economic personality"—or what is often called "economic man" as a result of the economic age we are living in at present. The second is "the specialist personality"—or "specialist man"—which derives directly from the concept of economic man ever since Adam Smith made a compelling case for specialization in his popular book *The Wealth of Nations* published in 1776 that was devoted to demonstrating in concrete terms how it is possible to maximize human productivity and economic growth. Despite this, there are major problems with both these personality types that make it impossible to embrace them as viable role models for human action and behaviour in the future, despite the incredible impact they have had on human nature and behaviour over the last two centuries and still at present.

The principal problem with "the economic personality" is that the individual is seen largely as a commodity rather than a person and consequently a maximizer of consumer satisfaction in the marketplace. While this may provide a realistic portrait of how most people are treated by modern economic systems and the actual functioning of societies and marketplaces, the principle problem with this personality type is that it relates to one dimension of the individual's life only, albeit a very essential one. As Marx and others pointed out more than a century ago, it treats people as economic objects rather than human subjects to be exploited and manipulated in the interests of profit-making and economic growth.

Many of these same objections apply to "the specialist personality." Just as economic systems and labour practices are highly specialized in the modern world, so individuals are expected to specialize in the development of a narrow range of practical skills and a specific production function that is saleable in the marketplace. The problem here is that economic systems are changing so rapidly at the present time that these skills and abilities are often outdated or redundant soon after they were acquired, thereby leaving the individual at the mercy of powerful producers and the marketplace. To this should be added the fact that both these personality types yield a vision of the individual person that is compartmentalized, unidimensional, acquisitive, and incomplete, thereby revealing that it would be foolhardy to predicate personality development and behavior on either of these personality types in the future.

There is one other area where clues may be found that are helpful in uncovering solutions to these problems. It is the historical literature. Fortunately, there exists in the historical literature a wealth of insights into the nature and functioning of the human personality, the role of the individual in society and the world, and the character of the contemporary predicament facing all people and humanity as a whole. Much of this literature is religious, philosophical, and psychological in nature.

In the religious realm, for instance, there are all the teachings and historical writings of Christianity, Islam, Buddhism, Hinduism, Judaism, Confucianism, and numerous others. One only has to look at the Bible, the Talmud, the Q'uran, the Upanishads, the Sayings of

Confucius, or any other sacred texts to realize how full all these religions and religious writings are with valuable insights into human behaviour in a variety of social settings and geographical situations. These insights are multiplied many times over when the focus is shifted to the philosophical literature. From Plato, Aristotle, and Socrates down through Descartes, Locke, Hume, and Goethe to Husserl, Heidigger, Sartre, Russell, and countless others, a significant portion of the philosophical literature of every culture has been devoted to an understanding of the trials and tribulations of the individual and his or her roles and responsibilities in the world. Finally, and perhaps most importantly, a very substantial segment of the psychological literature from Freud and Jung and numerous contemporaries has been concerned with the problems of the individual, not only as an individual but also as a member of a community, society, social group, or country. While much of this literature seems to raise more questions than it answers at the present time, as indicated earlier, there is little doubt that eventually it will cast a great deal of light on the way individuals can deal effectively with the demands and dictates of a rapidly changing and quickly transforming world.

While all of this literature is enormously helpful in enabling people to cope with the vicissitudes and vagaries of modern life, it is not without its problems. In the first place, it is extremely diverse and diffuse. It exists in so many different places and locations that it is difficult to pin down and pull together in a way that provides a prototype of the human personality that is consistent with contemporary experience and reality. Secondly, much of this literature is designed to deal more with abnormal rather than normal behaviour, or with particular problems and highly esoteric areas of personality development. As a result, not enough of it is focused on the general problem of gleaning a clear impression and understanding of the average individual or human being and his or her roles and responsibilities in the modern world. Thirdly, this literature is often more appropriate to the past than it is to the present and the future. For example, many of the most important religious, philosophical, and psychological writings and teachings that deal with the individual person are more in tune with a world that is very different from the world we are living in today. In a world characterized by profound secular and sacred change, unprecedented population growth in absolute terms, extraterrestrial discoveries, and huge communications, technological, and social developments, much of the literature that has been written about the human personality seems to be of limited usefulness in coming to grips with the types of problems people are encountering today or may be expected to encounter in the years and decades ahead. *While we must be exceedingly careful not to reject this indispensable source of knowledge, wisdom, insight, and understanding, we must be equally careful to ensure that it is consistent and relevant to the needs and requirements of people in the present and the future.*

While there is an incredible amount to be learned from all this literature, what is needed more than ever at this critical juncture in world history is a *new* prototype of the human personality. Such a prototype must be capable of coming to grips with the realities and problems of the present and the prospects and possibilities of the future.

Of all the places where fragments can be found that are helpful in piecing together this prototype, culture possesses more than its share of possibilities. This is because culture has contained within it the depth of understanding and breadth of vision that is necessary to illuminate a vital and viable path to the future. As a result, it is through deeper and deeper forays into the realm of culture that we are able to slowly but surely piece together a portrait of the human personality that possesses many of the most essential qualities, capabilities, and characteristics that are needed to confront the numerous problems of the present and the unlimited opportunities of the future. It is to this matter that attention can now be directed.

Chapter Two
The Concept of the Cultural Personality

The cultural personality is a compound term. It derives its substance and significance from two of the most dynamic, compelling, and evocative concepts imaginable, namely personality and culture. Since both these concepts contain a panorama of different meanings rather than a single meaning,[2] it is necessary to examine these meanings very carefully first, and then fuse them together to stand face to face with the concept of the cultural personality.

First, there is the concept of personality. Like the concept of culture, it has a long and distinguished history. In fact, it can be traced back to ancient times, to the Greeks and Romans and their use of the term *persona,* from which the modern term personality is derived.

In its original form, persona was the term that was used to denote the masks that were used in Greek and Roman dramas. These masks, which were adaptations of the masks of comedy and tragedy and had horns in the mouthpiece to amplify the sound, were used to distinguish the role of the actor or actress. Interestingly, this led to a fundamental division between the two basic dimensions of personality: the real self which is more internal in nature; and the role the individual plays in society which is more external in nature. It is a division that has persisted right up to the present day. Whether

2. Gordon Allport, *Pattern and Growth in Personality* (New York: Holt, Rinehart and Winston, 1963), and Alfred Kroeber and Clyde Kluckhohn, *Culture: A Critical Review of Concepts and Definitions* (New York: Vintage Books, 1952).

it is the individual seen in terms of a subjective-objective split, the self and the other, the introvert and the extrovert, the egoist and the altruist, or any other dichotomous division, this basic separation between the internal and external dimensions of the personality, which can often be in conflict with one another, has been a basic preoccupation of personality theory.

This same split is manifested in the differences between the concepts of personality and character: the former being viewed as more external and socially and environmentally oriented, and the latter being viewed as more internal and morally and spiritually oriented. Gordon Allport explains this split in terms of the original Latin and Greek meanings of the two terms, as well as their subsequent impact on American and European psychology:

> No less fascinating than the term *personality* is the term *character*. The two are often used interchangeably, although the first is of Latin derivation, the second of Greek, meaning engraving. It is the mark of a man [woman]—his [her]pattern of traits or his [her] life-style.... European psychologists, however, seem to have a preference for *character*, while American psychologists favour *personality*. There is an interesting reason for the difference.... The former term (personality) suggests appearance, visible behaviour, surface quality; the latter (character) suggests deep (perhaps inborn), fixed, and basic structure. Now American psychology has a preference for environmentalism; its behavioristic leaning leads it to stress outer movement, visible action. European psychology, on the other hand, tends to stress what is inborn in the nature of man [woman], what is deeply etched and relatively unchanging.[3]

3. Ibid., pp. 30–32 (inserts mine).

This same distinction is evident in occidental and oriental philosophy. While there are obviously many exceptions, generally speaking occidental philosophy has been externally and environmentally oriented, concerned largely with asserting human and technological dominance and control over nature. Oriental philosophy, on the other hand, has been more internally and spiritually oriented, concerned primarily with exploring those deep caverns and mysterious spaces that exist within people. In the vernacular of American and European psychology, the occidental preoccupation suggests a greater focus on "personality" whereas the oriental preoccupation suggests a greater focus on "character."

Over the last two thousand years, both "personality" and "character" have acquired a variety of meanings. These meanings are very much in evidence in most disciplines, but particularly in philosophy, theology, law, sociology, and psychology. In philosophy, for example, personality has been used as a synonym for selfhood, especially as it relates to the idea of perfection and something of supreme value. In theology, both character and personality are conspicuous: character referring to an individual of good moral standing or worth; and personality referring to members of the trinity, that is, the three forms of appearance or persons in the same essence. In law, personality is often used to refer to any individual enjoying legal status, either separately or as a member of a social or community group. And in the therapeutic arts and sciences, personality is generally deemed to be the sum total of all inborn or acquired traits and characteristics.

With the advent of modern psychology and psychoanalysis, interest in the notions of personality and character intensified considerably, so much so that Jan

Christiaan Smuts recommended the creation of a new discipline called "Personology" to deal with this:

> As the key to all the highest interests of the human race, Personality seems to be quite the most important and fruitful problem to which the thinkers of the coming generation could direct their attention. In Personality will probably be found the answer to some of the hardest and oldest questions that have troubled the heart as well as the head of man [woman]. The problem of Personality seems as hard as it is important. Not without reason have thinkers throughout the ages shied off from it. But it holds precious secrets for those who will seriously devote themselves to the new science or discipline of Personology.[4]

With the growing interest in personality has come a renewed interest in the discrepancy between the "essence" of the individual and his or her "role" in society. Regardless of whether it is Freud, Adler, Jung, Maslow, Allport, Linton, or other scholars, concerted attempts have been made to understand how and why individuals "behave" the way they do, as well as how they go about organizing their lives to form an overall pattern. Psychologists and psychiatrists often liken this process to the peeling of an onion, whereby the successive layers or "roles" of the individual are progressively removed until the real self is revealed.

Throughout this book, the term personality will be used to embrace both the essence and the role, or the internal and external dimensions, of the individual. In other words, character will be viewed as a component, albeit an exceedingly important component, of personality. While this is somewhat inconsistent with the

4. Jan Christiaan Smuts, *Holism and Evolution* (New York: The Viking Press, 1926), p. 289 (insert mine).

scholarly literature, and particularly the historical separation between personality and character, it is consistent with the all-embracing meaning the term personality is acquiring in the modern world. For example, in his book *The Cultural Background of Personality*, Ralph Linton defines personality as "the organized aggregate of psychological processes and states pertaining to the individual."[5] In a similar fashion, Gordon Allport defines personality as "the dynamic organization within the individual of those psychophysical systems that determine his [her] characteristic behaviour and thought."[6]

The following definition from the *Encyclopaedia Britannica* serves a useful purpose in this regard, since it brings out many of the fundamental properties and features of personality we will be concerned with in this book:

> the unique organization of psychophysical traits or characteristics, inherent and acquired, that distinguish each individual and are observable in his [her] relations to the environment and to the social group.[7]

This definition serves a valuable purpose in many ways. First, it emphasizes the psychophysical traits and characteristics that distinguish each person and are observable in his or her conduct. In so doing, it embraces the mental, emotional, physical, and spiritual dimensions of the human personality and places the focus directly on the ways of thinking, feeling, acting, behaving, belonging, and especially being that are basic to the personality of every individual. Second, it empha-

5. Ralph Linton, *The Cultural Background of Personality* (New York: Appleton-Century Crofts, 1945), p. 84.
6. Allport, *Pattern and Growth*, p. 28 (insert mine).
7. *The New Encyclopaedia Britannica* (Chicago: Encyclopaedia Britannica Inc., 1989), p. 311 (insert mine).

sizes the distinctiveness of every person, since, in the final analysis, every human being is "one of a kind" as manifested by his or her actions, attitudes, beliefs, patterns, values, and ways of perceiving the world. Third, it emphasizes the organization of all the traits and characteristics of the individual, both inherent and exhibited, thereby suggesting that there is some internal process of evaluating and ordering going on as well as some central organizing principle or principles around which people orchestrate their behaviour. And finally, it takes into account both the internal and external dimensions of the human personality, particularly as they relate to the self as well as to other human beings and the world at large. Momentarily we will have an opportunity to probe more deeply into these attributes and characteristics. Here, however, suffice it to say that they are of utmost importance to the notion of the cultural personality.

If personality is a difficult concept to pin down, so is culture, perhaps even more so. For like personality, culture possesses a long history of different meanings and numerous definitions. Consequently, whatever definition or meaning of culture is employed is bound to have a profound effect on the personality prototype derived from it.

A review of the literature suggests that there is a vast array of different definitions of culture that could be used to form the foundations for the cultural personality.[8] Fortunately, these definitions can be classified according to the basic theme that is inherent in them. This makes it possible to reduce a very unwieldy number of definitions to a much more manageable set of "concepts" of culture. For present purposes, the most relevant of these concepts are the philosophical, artistic,

8. Kroeber and Kluckhohn, *Culture*.

humanistic, anthropological, and cosmological.[9] Interestingly, each of these concepts corresponds to a very specific time period: ancient and medieval; renaissance; romantic; modern; and post modern. It pays to examine each of these concepts in turn, not only because they provide the historical antecedents and theoretical foundations on which the cultural personality is predicated, but also because they contain the clues that are necessary and invaluable in unlocking the secrets of the personality prototype we are endeavouring to uncover and clarify.

The philosophical concept of culture is by far the oldest. It derives from Roman times, and particularly Cicero who said, "culture is the philosophy or cultivation of the soul." Clearly Cicero's intention was to equate culture with the highest development of the individual. What is interesting to note for present purposes is not only the emphasis on the highest development of all, but also the emphasis on culture as a process of cultivation. It is a process of cultivation that requires constant nurturing and attention, as well as the proper nutrients and ingredients, if it is to grow, mature, ripen, and flourish properly.

The advantages of this specific concept of culture for the cultural personality are obvious. By focusing attention on the highest development of the individual, it places the spotlight squarely on one of the most important personality prerequisites, namely the need to develop all the capabilities of the individual, and with them, the ability to think clearly, feel deeply, care strongly, and so forth. In a world where this is far too often cloudy and confused, this obviously represents a very essential dimension of personality development.

9. D. Paul Schafer, *The Character of Culture* (Scarborough, ON: World Culture Project, 1989).

Like the philosophical concept, the artistic concept has a long history. It can also be traced back to ancient times, but especially to the Renaissance, where culture was equated with the Muses, especially those of epic and lyric poetry, music, tragedy, sacred song, dance, and comedy. This concept of culture is still very much in vogue in most parts of the world today.

Whereas the emphasis in the philosophical concept is on the development of the soul or highest capabilities of people, the emphasis in the artistic concept is on the development of the aesthetic capabilities of people. Clearly this brings into play a more specific but equally broad range of skills and abilities, since the development of people's aesthetic capabilities requires not only mental ability, but also sensory, emotional, and spiritual abilities. The object here is not so much internal development but, rather, external development, since it requires the creation and presentation of works of art that can be shared with other people.

When culture is defined in artistic or aesthetic terms, it brings to the fore two dimensions of the personality that are of fundamental importance for the future. The first is creativity. Without doubt, the development of people's creative abilities is of vital importance, regardless of their profession, occupation, or station in life. Clearly it is going to take a great deal more originality, inventiveness, and ingenuity, that is to say more creativity, on the part of every person to live in a world characterized by revolutionary and pervasive change. But if it is essential to develop people's creativity to the fullest, it is also essential to develop their aesthetic sensitivities and sensibilities, as well as the ability to express pent-up feelings and emotions. For given the stresses and strains of modern life, it is clear that individuals who are not sensitive to the dynamic changes going on in the world around them or are incapable of expressing their innermost feelings and emotions, will increasingly turn to negative and more destructive forms of expressing and venting their frustrations.

Following closely on the heels of the artistic concept of culture is the humanistic concept. Here, culture is viewed not so much as the arts, but rather philosophy, literature, history, the arts, sciences, and indeed, the entire legacy from the past or the tangible and intangible cultural heritage of humankind. In an historical sense, the principal exponent of this broader, more humanistic view of culture was Matthew Arnold, the nineteenth-century British scholar, educator, and social critic.

For Arnold, culture was the pursuit of perfection, or, as he termed it, "the cultivation of sweetness and light." It was sweetness and light that was acquired through the relentless quest for knowledge, wisdom, understanding, and erudition. Such a quest must always be dynamic rather than static, "a growing and becoming rather than a having and a resting." This state of steadily-evolving perfection is best achieved, according to Arnold, through the harmonious development of all the faculties that comprise human nature:

> perfection—as culture, from a thorough disinterested study of human nature and human experience learns to conceive it—*is a harmonious expansion of all the powers which make the beauty and worth of human nature, and is not consistent with the over-development of any one power at the expense of the rest.* Here culture goes beyond religion, as religion is generally conceived by us.… It is in making endless additions to itself, in the endless expansion of its powers, in the endless growth

in wisdom and beauty, that the spirit of the human race finds its ideal. To reach this ideal, culture is an indispensable aid, and that is the true value of culture.[10]

Just as Arnold felt that culture should be seen in a dynamic rather than static way, so he believed that culture should be understood as an *active* rather than *passive* endeavour. While cultivation of sweetness and light tends to suggest a process that depends more on acquisition than action, absorption rather than giving, Arnold was careful to point out that this should merely be the first step in a long process of events aimed at taking sweetness and light - or the arts and education as we would say today—out of the hands of the elite and sharing it with the whole of humanity. As an educator, he felt very strongly that society had an obligation to provide the best possible education to the largest number of people:

> the moment culture is considered not merely as the endeavour to *see* and *learn* this, but as the endeavour, also, to make it *prevail*, the moral, social, and beneficent character of culture becomes manifest ... it knows that the sweetness and light of the few must be imperfect until the raw and unkindled masses of humanity are touched with sweetness and light....
>
> Men [women] of culture are the true apostles of equality. The great men [women] of culture are those who have had a passion for diffusing, for making prevail, for carrying from one end of society to the other, the best knowledge, the best ideas of their time; who have laboured to divest knowledge of all that was harsh, uncouth, difficult, abstract, professional, exclusive; to humanize it, to make it efficient outside the clique of

10. Matthew Arnold, *Culture and Anarchy* (Cambridge: Cambridge University Press, 1955,) pp. 47–48 (italics mine).

the cultivated and learned, yet still remaining the *best* knowledge and thought of the time, and a true source, therefore, of sweetness and light.[11]

If the humanistic concept of culture has much to recommend it, so does the anthropological concept. In a conceptual sense, the breakthrough here came when Sir Edward Burnett Tylor, one of the world's first anthropologists if not *the* first, broke with the long tradition of defining culture as the development of the soul, the arts, the humanities, or the finer things in life, and started defining culture as everything that is created and experienced by and in a society. In his *Origins of Culture*, published in 1871, Tylor penned what has since become the classic definition of culture:

> Culture, or civilization, taken in its widest ethnographic sense, is that *complex whole* which includes knowledge, belief, art, morals, law, custom, and any other capabilities and habits acquired by man [woman] as a member of society.[12]

Ever since it was first propounded, this far more expansive and all-inclusive way of looking at and defining culture has had a profound effect on scholarly and popular thinking. Directly or indirectly, this has contributed to two fundamental and seminal developments that have the greatest implications for the cultural personality and the future. First, it has contributed to the shift that has taken place from an absolute to a relative view of culture. Ever since Tylor, and following him Boas, Mead, Benedict, and many others, cultural values and practices have been deemed to be both relative and

11. Ibid., pp. 46, 69, 70 (inserts mine).
12. Edward Burnett Tylor, *The Origins of Culture* (New York: Harper and Row Publishers, 1958), p. 1 (italics and insert mine).

absolute, a function of a specific time and place as well as an idealized set of qualities or ideals. Second, and equally important for our purposes, the anthropological perception of culture has contributed substantially to a holistic or all-encompassing view of culture. Whereas all previous concepts of culture prior to Tylor's time were partial concepts, notes in a composition so to speak, here at last was an all-embracing concept and understanding of culture. This is where the concept of culture really starts to get interesting for purposes of the cultural personality.

So evocative and compelling has the anthropological concept of culture been that more and more public leaders, professional groups, and scholars are falling prey to its power. This was confirmed recently when the member states of UNESCO unanimously endorsed the following definition of culture at the Second World Conference on Cultural Policy in Mexico City in 1982:

> Culture ought to be considered today the collection of distinctive traits, spiritual and material, intellectual and affective, which characterize a society or social group. It comprises, besides arts and letters, modes of life, human rights, value systems, traditions and beliefs.[13]

This view that culture is the totality of human and societal experiences and not a specific or a few dimensions of it is rapidly gaining ground and working its way into popular thinking. When people talk about being "the products of their culture" today, they mean they are the products not only of their educational and artistic activities as Arnold defined it, or of the highest development and cultivation of the soul, as Cicero defined

13. UNESCO, *Mexico Declaration on Culture* (Mexico City and Paris: UNESCO, 1982 and 1983).

it. Rather, they mean they are the products of every-thing that exists in their society, including economic practices, political processes, social realities, religious institutions, technological developments, and all other elements and ingredients that go into making up their culture. In other words, they mean they are the products of what Tylor and others called "their culture as a whole," or "the complex whole."

We could go a long way towards embracing this significantly broader concept of culture if it was not for one fundamental problem. It is a problem that has to do with the way in which Tylor and other anthropologists perceived and defined "the whole."

It would be foolhardy in today's world to embrace any concept of culture which does not open up a commanding place for the natural environment at its very core. And herein lies the problem, not only with Tylor's concept of culture, but also with virtually every anthropological conception of culture since that time. Either nature is ignored entirely as standing outside the domain of culture, or it is tacitly assumed to provide the overall container within which culture is situated. In either case, it yields a concept of culture which, despite its numerous attractions and emphasis on the whole rather than the parts of the whole, is not consistent with the ecological reality of the situation that exists throughout the world today.

It is easy to see how anthropologists fell into the trap of becoming so preoccupied with the human species and its creations that they ignored, implicitly assumed, or took for granted the realm of nature. After all, anthropology is by definition concerned with the output and activities of human beings and the human species; it is left to other disciplines such as biology, botany, zoology, ecology, and so forth to concern themselves with the natural environment and the comings and goings of other species. Moreover, through the progressive development of technology, which many believe is the crowning achievement of the human species, it is often assumed that nature can eventually be brought under human control and humankind can be liberated from its age-old dependency on nature and the natural environment. Given these assumptions, it is easy to understand why some people believe that nature will eventually be eliminated entirely from the cultural equation.

In retrospect, it is apparent how erroneous these assumptions are and have been. For one thing, nature is obviously not going to be brought under human control, as recent developments throughout the world confirm as a result of global warming and other environmental changes and catastrophes. For another, technology is having a devastating effect on the natural environment. Under these circumstances, it is clear that nature and the natural environment cannot be assumed or taken for granted in the cultural equation any longer. On the contrary, they must be confronted head on and fully incorporated and integrated into the cultural equation. This can easily be confirmed by looking at any African, Asian, Latin American, European, North American, or Middle Eastern culture or country. Even the most cursory or superficial examination of these cultures will reveal that nature and the natural environment are, and always will be, active and indispensable agents in cultural change. In fact, it is through continuous, intensive, and vigorous interaction with the natural environment that all cultures originate and develop. It is this fact, more than any other, that makes it imperative to examine one more concept of culture.

This is the cosmological concept of culture. Seen in its most elementary form, the cosmological concept of culture treats culture as an "ordered whole" or "worldview."[14] While at first blush this specific concept of culture seems to share certain similarities with the anthropological concept, on closer inspection it is different in two very important respects. Whereas Tylor and other anthropologists defined "the whole" in such a way that it either excludes or takes for granted the entire realm of nature, the cosmological concept of culture defines "the whole" as everything that exists in the universe—animal, vegetable, and mineral as well as human. This all-embracing understanding of the whole, or what some prefer to call the "cosmic whole." includes not only the human species but all other species such as plants and animals as well as all matter with which the human species cohabits the universe. Perhaps Goethe expressed this best when he said, "he who wills the highest, must will the whole; he who treats of the spirit must presuppose and include nature."[15]

It is not only a different perception of "the whole" that differentiates the cosmological concept of culture from the anthropological concept. Whereas the focus of the anthropological concept is on the *complexity* of the whole, largely for the purpose of differentiating between different degrees of cultural sophistication, the focus of the cosmological concept is on how the whole is *ordered* or *organized.* In other words, the preoccupation of the cosmological conception of culture is with the values, value systems, and central organizing principle or principles that determine how the whole is structured and

14. Schafer, *Character*, pp. 27–61.
15. R. King, ed., *Goethe on Human Creativeness and other Goethe Essays* (Athens, Georgia: University of Georgia Press, 1950), p. xiii.

put together. It is this fact which gives the cosmological concept of culture its concern with "worldview," or the way in which cultures are not only composed but also position themselves in the world. Pierre Pascallon explains:

> Every culture, every people, every society must [discover and] rediscover its own interior cosmology, must arrive at a coherent account of its being in the world, must be able to locate itself in a recognizable world and find for itself the organizing principle of its world.[16]

It is clear from the foregoing that a very specific personality type is inherent in each of the concepts of culture we have examined. For example, the philosophical concept produces people concerned with the development of the soul. Here, as we observed earlier, the emphasis is on one's internal development, essence, and state of being. Similarly, the artistic concept produces the artist. Here, the emphasis is on the development of one's sensorial, emotional, and aesthetic capabilities. Likewise, the humanistic concept produces the humanist, or the "cultured" person. In this case, the emphasis is on familiarity with the legacy from the past, and with it, cultivation of the capacity for refined judgement and critical discrimination.

Each of these three personality types possesses certain attributes that are essential to the overall understanding of the cultural personality. By endorsing the need to develop and cultivate the soul, and to react creatively, imaginatively, and compassionately in a variety of situations and circumstances, these three personality types contain specific clues that are helpful in unlock-

16. Pierre Pascallon, "The Cultural Dimension of Development," *Intereconomics*. January/February, 1986, p. 7 (insert mine).

ing the many diverse secrets of the cultural personality. Nevertheless, they all suffer from one very obvious drawback. They all represent partial, restrictive, or limited approaches to what is essentially a multidimensional, open-ended, and limitless process. No one understood this type of problem better than T. S. Eliot:

> We may be thinking of learning and a close acquaintance with accumulated wisdom of the past: if so, our man [woman] of culture is the scholar. We may be thinking of philosophy in the widest sense—an interest in, and some ability to manipulate, abstract ideas: if so, we may mean the intellectual.... Or we may be thinking of the arts: if so, we mean the artist and the amateur or dilettante. But what we seldom have in mind is all of these things at the same time. We do not find, for instance, that an understanding of music or painting figures explicitly in Arnold's description of the cultured man: yet no one will deny that these attainments play a part in culture....
>
> People are always ready to consider themselves persons of culture, on the strength of one proficiency, when they are not only lacking in others, but blind to those they lack. An artist of any kind, even a very great artist, is not for this reason alone a man [woman] of culture: artists are not only often insensitive to other arts than those which they practice, but sometimes have very bad manners or meagre intellectual gifts. The person who contributes to culture, however important his [her] contribution may be, is not always a "cultured person."[17]

The anthropological concept of culture helped immeasurably here. By defining culture in a much more expansive way, it broadened the orbit of culture

17. T. S. Eliot. *Notes Towards the Definition of Culture* (London: Faber and Faber, 1963), pp. 22–23 (inserts mine).

far beyond philosophy, the arts, or the legacy from the past to include virtually every domain of life, from eating to sleeping, work to leisure, and ideals and ideologies to commonplace ideas and realities.

When the anthropological concept of culture is applied to the individual, the resulting personality type is "the complex whole." This has a number of advantages over the previous personality types, since it focuses attention on the whole person and the totality of human experience, not some limited part of it. Here, the individual is seen as the sum total of all the economic, social, political, aesthetic, humanistic, recreational, and philosophical experiences encountered in life, not as the product of a highly specialized set of skills, experiences, or abilities. Moreover, the individual is also seen as being complex, which is as it should be in view of the myriad experiences which punctuate his or her life.

While this personality type has a great deal to recommend it, it also breaks down as a prototype capable of guiding human behaviour in the future. And it does so for precisely the same reason that the anthropological concept of culture breaks down as a concept for explaining the total character of culture. Not only is it too human centred and therefore incapable of embracing nature and the natural environment as an integral and indispensable dimension of all cultural life, but also it places the focus on the complexity of the human personality which, despite its relevance to the nature of contemporary life, is not the most essential requirement for effective personality development in the years and decades ahead.

When the cosmological concept of culture is used as the basis for the human personality, the resulting personality type is the whole person as an "ordered whole" as indicated earlier. In this case, the emphasis is squarely where it belongs: on the cosmic character of the whole, as well as on the way in which all the component parts of the whole—or culture—are combined to form a harmonious and integrated entity.

Clearly this personality type is not the philosopher, the artist, the humanist, or even the individual as "a complex whole." Nor is it a new age person, or updated version of "renaissance man." Rather, it is a personality type concerned first and foremost with the way in which all the various component parts of being are galvanized and coalesced to form a coherent and integrated unity that includes the natural environment and nature. In the final analysis, isn't this really what personality development is all about? Despite what many modern economic, political, educational, and technological leaders would have us believe, aren't we and shouldn't we be concerned with blending together all of life's infinite ingredients and experiences in such a way that they form a total tapestry or seamless web?

A person's total worldview is a quintessential aspect of this. For just as every culture exudes a worldview which is based on its unique structure, location, and outlook on the world and nature, so every individual possesses a worldview that is based on his or her unique personality, position, and outlook on the universe. Robert Redfield expressed this most effectively when he said:

> "World view" attends especially to the way a man [woman], in a particular society, sees himself [herself] in relation to all else. It is the properties of existence as distinguished from and related to the self. It is, in short, a man's [woman's] idea of the universe. It is that organization of ideas which answers to a man [woman]

the questions: Where am I? Among what do I move? What are my relations to these things?[18]

Questions as fundamental as this are surely the most important questions of all. Not only are they the questions that every person must confront regardless of his or her station in life or geographical location in the world, but also they are questions that lie at the very heart of the human condition.

It was questions like these that Albert Schweitzer had in mind when he talked about the importance of a personal worldview and the need for *elemental thinking*. For Schweitzer, not only do all people manifest their worldview in the way they choose to live their lives and express themselves in their works and deeds, but also they are all compelled to wrestle with a vast series of fundamental questions concerned with the meaning of life and their role, responsibilities, and purpose in the world:

> Elemental thinking is that which starts from the fundamental questions about the relations of man [woman] to the universe, about the meaning of life, and about the nature of goodness. It stands in the most immediate connection with the thinking which impulse stirs in everyone. It enters into that thinking, widening and deepening it.[19]

While the cultural personality is concerned with addressing all the specific, practical, and commonplace questions that must be addressed in life, such as where to live, what to work at, who to live with, whether to

18. Anthony C. Wallace, *Culture and Personality* (New York: Random House, 1967), p. 99 (inserts mine).
19. Charles R. Roy, ed., *Albert Schweitzer: An Anthology* (Boston: The Beacon Press, 1947), p. 4 (insert mine).

have children or not, and when to retire, there is a realization that these questions are fundamentally related to broader, deeper, and more essential and profound questions connected to the individual's worldview. It is for this reason that the cultural personality is concerned with the nature of reality and the fundamental meaning and purpose of life, as well as what one sees when one looks outward onto the universe and inward into the self.

In the end, the cultural personality is concerned with the whole person in this broader, deeper, and more fundamental sense. Despite the importance of this particular personality type for the present and the future, unfortunately we seem to be moving farther and farther away from it rather than closer and closer to it. And herein lies the problem. The dictates and demands of contemporary life and the modern world are such that they are causing people everywhere in the world to become more and more caught up with the superficialities of life and less and less concerned with those fundamental and profound needs that are the essence of life itself. The further we get away from the idea of the whole person in this all-encompassing, cosmological sense, the more fractured and fragmented our lives become. It is as if our lives, like our personalities, are being pulled and stretched in so many different directions that we have lost our ability to unify them and give them meaning.

Many may think that the cosmological concept of the individual as an ordered whole is a new idea. Perhaps it is in some respects. However, in many other respects, it is very old. It can be traced back to ancient times, to the Greeks and their preoccupation with "the kosmos" or "the universe as an ordered whole," as well as with "the logos," or the discourse or logic behind how the whole is structured, put together, and integrated into a single entity. Whereas the Greeks were concerned with the universe as an ordered whole, our concern is with the person as an ordered whole. It is time to delve into this most important matter more deeply.

Chapter Three
The Characteristics of the Cultural Personality

The time has come to put some flesh on the bare bones of the cultural personality. What do we mean by this captivating concept in fact? What are its most fundamental characteristics?

While there are many characteristics that give the cultural personality its shape and identity, in the final analysis the cultural personality is *holistic, centred, authentic, unique, creative, altruistic,* and, last but far from least, *humane.* Let us examine each of these characteristics in turn. In the process, flesh will start to appear on the bare bones of the cultural personality.

First and foremost, the cultural personality is holistic. By this is meant that the cultural personality is constantly striving to combine all the component parts of being together to form a comprehensive and integrated entity. To achieve this according to Jan Christiaan Smuts is to achieve the highest state of personality development:

> Personality then is a new whole, is the highest and completest of all wholes, is the most recent conspicuous mutation in the evolution of Holism.... [It is] the supreme embodiment of Holism both in its individual and its universal tendencies. It is the final synthesis of all the operative factors in the universe into unitary wholes, and both in its unity and its complexity it constitutes the great riddle of the universe.[20]

To be holistic is to be constantly attempting to see,

20. Smuts, *Holism*, p. 263 (insert mine).

feel, experience, and comprehend the unity or one-ness of all things and being, or, as Goethe espoused it, "to live in the whole." It matters little that holism in some ultimate, metaphysical sense may be unat-tainable; it is always possible to add new information, insights, perceptions, and ideas to the ever-expanding dimensions of the whole. What is important is to be continuously and systematically engaged *in the quest* to achieve this ideal, and to this end, relentlessly acting to fuse the mental, physical, emotional, spiritual, and all other aspects of being together to form a seamless web. Ultimately, this is what the cultural personality is really all about. It is about perpetual acts of integration and synthesis aimed at melding all the diverse fragments of being or existence together—internal and external, subjective and objective, material and non-material, the self and the other—to form a harmonious whole. John Cowper Powys recognized the crucial importance of this when he said:

> The whole purpose and end of culture is a thrilling happiness of a particular sort—of the sort, in fact, that is caused by a response to life made by a harmony of the intellect, the imagination, and the senses.[21]

Just as the cultural personality is engaged in the constant search to discover the inherent wholeness of the self as well as in the world, so it is constantly striving to recognize this same wholeness in others. For the cultural personality, people are not defined by their colour, age, race, creed, profession, status, or any other single characteristic. Rather they are defined in terms of their wholeness, taking into account all their

21. John Cowper Powys, *The Meaning of Culture* (New York:W.W. Norton and Company Inc., 1929), p. 77.

diverse attributes, strengths, weaknesses, and frailties. In other words, they are defined as total human beings and treated as such. If judgements are to be made at all, they should always be made in terms of the whole person and never in terms of one or two highly selective traits or distinguishing characteristics.

Since holism is in effect "the tendency in nature to form wholes that are more than the sum of the parts by creative evolution,"[22] it is appropriate to ask what it is that makes the whole greater than the parts and the sum of its parts for the cultural personality. This "extra something" has been variously described as a value system, a soul, a spirit, or a philosophy of life. Since it is through this process that the cultural personality becomes centred in the world as well as in the self, it requires some explanation.

As with personality development of any type, the starting point for the development of the cultural personality is with life's everyday and multifarious experiences. These experiences are not only exceedingly diverse, but also they are largely undifferentiated. They invade the individual at all times, as well as from many different directions.

With the passing of time, the cultural personality begins to make associations and connections between the myriad experiences that are encountered in everyday life. These associations and connections form the basis of values, since they involve comparisons between one type of experience and another. Here is where assessments are made of life's different encounters, and priorities are established between and among these encounters, thereby making it possible to rank them accordingly in the overall scheme of things. Just how

22. *Concise Oxford Dictionary* (Oxford: Oxford University Press, 1965).

important culture is in this process of value formation was revealed by Mircea Malitza when he said, "culture is the crucible from which values emerge, where preferences are formed and the hierarchy among them is established."[23]

According to Albert Kroeber and Clyde Kluckhohn, values are important because they provide "foci for patterns of organization for the materials of culture ... and give significance to our understanding of cultures." They go on to observe:

> ... values provide the only basis for the fully intelligible comprehension of culture, because the actual organization of all cultures is primarily in terms of their values. This becomes apparent as soon as one attempts to present the picture of a culture without reference to its values.... The account becomes an unstructured, meaningless assemblage of items having relation to one another only through coexistence in locality and moment ... a mere laundry list.[24]

What is true for culture as well as for cultures is also true for the cultural personality. For just as there are collective values in the larger cultural sense, so there are personal values in a more restricted, individual sense. It is these values that help to give shape, substance, character, and integrity to the cultural personality.

Values make it possible for the cultural personality to sort out what is relevant from what is irrelevant, what is valuable from what is valueless, and what is meaningful from what is meaningless. Without this, as Kroeber and Kluckhohn rightly observe, life really does become little more than a laundry list, an assemblage of activities

23. Mircea Maltiza. "Culture and the New Order: A Pattern of Integration," *Cultures* 3: 4 (1976), p. 98.
24. Kroeber and Kluckhohn, *Culture*, pp. 340–41.

bearing little or no relationship to each other, let alone to the wider community within which they are situated. Without values, there is no means of separating truth from falsehood, good from evil, justice from injustice, morality from immorality.

For the cultural personality, there are three aspects to this question of values that require reflection and attention. The first is the conflict between personal and societal values. There are bound to be times when there are fundamental differences and conflicts between the personal values of the individual and the collective values of society, particularly in those areas where there may be limitations or shortcomings in societal values that the cultural personality is concerned with addressing. The second is the discrepancy between absolute and relative values, or values that are designed to manifest some sort of universal truth in contrast to values that are a function of a specific time or place as indicated earlier. Here, the cultural personality is careful to avoid falling into the trap of thinking that values for one person or country must necessarily be values for other people or other countries, or for all people and the world as a whole. And finally, the third is the realization that values must be constantly attended to if they are to be cultivated properly and effectively.

In the process of cultivating a viable set of personal values, the cultural personality becomes aware that values are not only essential elements in a fully-developed personality, but also sources of integrity and inspiration. As a result, they should be savoured and celebrated at every opportunity:

There is a sense in which the whole of human culture is a struggle towards the higher values. Can there be any greater expression of culture than art? Art surely lifts us up, although it would not be likely to exist without us... We were meant to actualize the higher values, and incidental to this task is the privilege of enjoying them.[25]

It is through the process of struggling to formulate, reformulate, and refine values that the cultural personality becomes aware of a deeper development that begins to take place in the fertile soil of the soul and the self. It has to do with the formulation of a set of central organizing principles around which personal values are galvanized and coalesced.

These central organizing principles may be based on love, beauty, truth, integrity, creativity, caring, or any other worthwhile human attribute. Since they are finely honed over a long period of time, they have a seasoned quality, stability, and solidarity about them. Nevertheless, no greater mistake could be made than to assume that they are fixed, immutable, and unchanging. On the contrary, they are constantly being broadened, deepened, and refined in order to remain in tune with the dynamic nature of reality and the internal character of the self. For just as the world is constantly producing new problems, challenges, and possibilities, so the cultural personality is constantly redefining and reformulating its central organizing principles in order to bring them into line with the ever-evolving needs of society and humanity.

It is important to emphasize that these central organizing principles are what make it possible for the cultural personality to feel rooted in the self, as well as flexible, adaptable, and responsive to the never-ending changes that are taking place in the world and humanity at large. By providing the fundamental focal points around which experiences and values are organized,

25. Feibleman, *Human Culture*, pp. 326–27.

arranged, and coalesced, these central organizing principles provide coherence, connectedness, and continuity in space and time. While they mature and ripen over time depending on individual needs and preferences, they nevertheless remain the benchmarks and touchstones that are imperative for the effective functioning of the cultural personality in the real world.

It is through the progressive refinement of these central organizing principles, or what some people call the creation of a viable "value system," that the cultural personality begins to fashion a very specific philosophy of life. In his book *Cosmic Understanding*, Milton Munitz explains why it is so essential to have such a philosophy:

> When acquired, such a philosophy provides a framework of basic principles that helps guide a person's reactions to the crises and opportunities of life, to the universal facts of human existence—being born and dying, being a member of society, being part of a wider universe. To have a set of basic guiding principles, whether accepted from some external source or worked out for oneself, is an inescapable requirement for a human being.[26]

What is significant about this philosophy for the cultural personality is how distinctive it is. Having taken the time and trouble to wrestle with all the diverse elements that go into making it, it could hardly be otherwise:

> A philosophy of one's own, grown tough and flexible amid the shocks of the world, is a far more important achievement than the ability to expound the precise differences between the great philosophic schools of thought....

26. Milton K. Munitz, *Cosmic Understanding* (Princeton: Princeton University Press,1986), p. 260.

The art of self-culture begins with a deeper awareness, borne in upon us either by some sharp emotional shock or little by little like an insidious rarefied air, of the marvel of our being alive at all; alive in a world as startling and mysterious, as lovely and horrible, as the one we live in. Self culture without some kind of *integrated* habitual manner of thinking is apt to fail us just when it is wanted the most. *To be a cultured person is to be a person with some kind of original philosophy.*[27]

It is through hammering out this philosophy that the cultural personality begins to comprehend what it means to be centred in the self as well as in the world. This is because there is a growing awareness of the fact that a central rudder has been created that provides strength, durability, and a clear sense of direction to the life course. John Cowper Powys uses a botanical illustration to drive this point home with startling clarity:

Slowly, as life tightens the knot of our inner being, our outer leaves, like those of a floating water-plant, expand in the sunshine and in the rain of pure chance; but we still are aware of the single stalk under the surface, of the single root that gives meaning to all.[28]

It is doubtful whether the cultural personality can ever become fully conscious of the single root that provides centredness in life and in the self without becoming "authentic" or true to oneself. It is this requirement that Thomas Carlyle had in mind when he penned his great law of culture:

Let each become all that he [she] was created capable of being; expand, if possible, to his [her] full growth;

27. Powys, *Meaning of Culture*, pp. 23, 8 (italics mine).
28. Ibid., p. 11.

resisting all impediments, casting off all foreign, especially all noxious adhesions; and show himself [herself] at length in his [her] own shape and stature, be these what they may.[29]

There are two aspects of this law that require our attention. First, there is the idea of the growth and development of the personality itself, not only in terms of the infinite expenditure of all those energies that are needed to achieve maturity and full growth, but also in terms of the struggle that must be constantly waged to achieve real authenticity. It is cast in the form of a struggle because that is precisely what it is; it is a struggle that must be continuously waged within the self as well as in the world to "become what thou art." To do so is to resist the pressures of imitation and conformity and compel oneself to come to grips with one's real essence and fundamental purpose in life. This is what John Calvin had in mind when he talked about fulfilling one's destiny or "calling," as well as what Joseph Campbell meant when he talked about "following our bliss," or never taking the easy way out but always striving to achieve one's full potential and what brings real purpose, meaning, and fulfillment in life.

This struggle to realize one's full potential is surely one of the most difficult challenges in life of all. It means plumbing the depths of our being to confront the real self and achieve genuine identity, rather than giving in to what others might wish us to be or succumbing to the dictates of convention and society. Such a challenge is totally independent of our station in life or geographical location in the world. It relates as much to the farmer in Africa, the corporate executive in Asia, and the landlord

29. Thomas Carlyle, *Critical and Miscellaneous Essays*, Vol. I (London: Clay and Taylor, Printers, 1869), p. 16 (inserts mine).

in Latin America as it does to the educator in North America and the politician in Europe.

But there is another aspect to Carlyle's great law of culture that also demands our attention. It has to do with the limits of authenticity: where one person's quest for authenticity ends and another person's begins. What happens, for instance, when one person's quest for authenticity impinges on, interferes with, or threatens the rights and freedoms of others? For Carlyle, this eventually spelled disaster for his great law of culture because it opened the doors to—and justified—the evil practices of dictators and not just the good deeds of humanitarians. However, for the cultural personality, this always sets in motion the search for an alternative path to authenticity—a way that preserves the right for authenticity without running roughshod over the needs, rights, privileges, and freedoms of other people or society as a whole. It is for this reason that the cultural personality always deals with everything in context rather than in isolation. The quest for authenticity is never used as a license for legitimizing whatever one wants in life, or for achieving one's own goals and objectives at the expense of others.

It is difficult to see how the cultural personality can achieve real authenticity in the world without becoming unique or one of a kind.

While it is often said that every individual in the world has a double living somewhere else in the world in a physical sense, this is certainly not true in a cultural sense. In a cultural sense, all people are different and unique. From the moment they enter the world, their lives are filled with a continuous flow of experiences, challenges, situations, and opportunities that are totally different from those of other people. Not only are there enormous variations in the way people interact with friends, family, relatives, colleagues, strangers, and the natural environment, but also there are significant differences in the myriad features and specific circumstances that govern their lives.

In the process of weaving together life's infinite elements to form an ordered whole, the cultural personality slowly but surely creates a life that is without duplication elsewhere in the world. This fact is worthy of a great deal of reflection. It should be celebrated in good times and bad, in moments of pleasure as well as in times of adversity. Not only does it speak volumes about the need that exists in every person to be distinctive and different in his or her own right—to have a personal identity and life differentiated from any other person—but also it supplies much of the fuel that is required to propel people to higher heights and levels of accomplishment.

It is the ability of the cultural personality to meld together life's innumerable fragments and elements to form a life that is distinctly different from that of any other person that makes the cultural personality not only unique, but also creative.

As profuse and unpredictable as life's events and experiences are, it is not the events and experiences themselves that make life a creative act. Rather, it is the way these events and experiences are spun together to form a coherent and comprehensive entity. For in the process of weaving together the infinite strands of life's untold mysteries and profundities, the cultural personality is compelled to exercise a great deal of creativity. It is creativity that derives from the inalienable right of all people to fashion life in accordance with the demands and dictates of their own needs, requirements, circumstances, and experiences. Every person, regardless of educational background, professional training, social situation, religious persuasion, or spiritual necessities has the right to fashion life in such a way that it is highly creative in its design, development, and execution.

While the type of creativity we are talking about here is not the kind of creativity that is usually limited to artists, scientists, and scholars, it is creativity nonetheless. It probably will never manifest itself in the production of great paintings, outstanding compositions, rare books, or famous inventions, that is to say, in the creation of works of art, science, or scholarship capable of withstanding the test of time. Nevertheless, it is still creativity, since it involves taking the infinite building blocks of life and arranging them in such a way that the result is a life without parallel or duplication elsewhere in the world.

It follows from this that life is dynamic and organic rather than static and fixed. As a result, it is in a constant state of evolutionary flux, not only in the way in which experiences and values are constantly being arranged and rearranged, but also in the way in which the central organizing principles and underlying philosophy of life is perpetually being enlarged, reformulated, and recreated. Ralph Linton, writing about the relationship between culture and personality, refers to this dynamic and organic property this way:

> Personalities are dynamic continuums, and although it is important to discover their content, organization and performance at a given point in time, it is still more important to discover the processes by which they develop, grow and change....[30]

> Each individual is born with a unique configuration of physical and psychological potentialities, and from the

30. Linton, *Cultural Background*, p. 3.

moment of birth finds himself [herself] in interaction with his [her] environment. *The process of personality development is one of continual assimilation and organization of the experiences which he [she] derives from this interaction.* As each new item of experience is integrated it becomes a factor in later interactions with the environment, and consequently in the production of new experience.[31]

It is this dynamic and organic property that renders to the cultural personality the ability to continuously adjust to a world that is in perpetual motion, as well as to confront whatever problems, challenges, and obstacles loom up in the way. This is especially important at the present time given all the major transformations that are going on in the world. Most important in terms of the future are all the economic and employment changes and challenges that are occurring in every part of the world today. While it was commonplace several decades ago for most people who were employed in the world to have a single job, occupation, and profession for a good part of their lives, this has all changed and changed dramatically in recent years. In today's world, most people will likely have ten to fifteen jobs over the course of their lives, and probably in very different occupations and professions. Add to this the changes that are taking place in technology, robotics, artificial intelligence, and the like and it is clear that all people will have to have a great deal more ingenuity as well as the ability to invent, innovate, and adapt much more readily and fully than people had in the past.

Not only will this require transformative changes in education, training, and learning, but also it will require

31. Francis L.K. Hsu, ed., *Aspects of Culture and Personality: A Symposium* (New York: Abelard-Schuman, 1954), p. 202 (italics and inserts mine).

the development of all the entrepreneurial skills and abilities that are necessary to make ends meet in the years and decades ahead. For the reality of the situation at present and prospects for the future indicate that the large majority of people in the world will likely have to create many of their own jobs and employment opportunities in the future. This will necessitate the cultivation of creativity and entrepreneurship to the greatest possible extent. It will also require people who are far more innovative than people in the past, thereby making the creative and entrepreneurial dimension of the cultural personality one of the most essential characteristics of personality development of all.

While it is important to develop creativity in the short run, it is even more imperative to develop it in the long run. For every person in the world must confront the fact that a kind of "psychological death" or "static malaise" can set in at any age or stage of life if the appropriate precautions are not taken to prevent it. Regardless of whether a person is in the prime of life, mid-career, early retirement, or the final stages of life's ever-unfolding mystery, there is the perpetual risk of becoming so mired in the muck of reality that it is impossible to extricate oneself and get back on course. If the creative and dynamic capabilities of the personality are not swung fully into play here, what may result is a deadening process that slowly but surely sucks every ounce of energy and enthusiasm out of the life process.

The cultural personality is not only fully aware of this but is constantly and methodically taking steps to overcome it. It does so by drawing on its own inner reserves and innovative abilities to ceaselessly create new challenges and opportunities for itself to a far greater extent. No sooner is one challenge met or opportunity seized than others are put in their place.

It is unlikely that the cultural personality can achieve this without acquiring one of the noblest characteristics of all. We are referring, of course, to altruism, or the ability to give to others and make commitments to causes that are greater than the self.

It was altruism that Matthew Arnold had in mind when he spoke about the need to take education and learning out of the hands of elites and share it with the whole of humanity. Likewise, it was altruism that Pitirim Sorokin had in mind when he penned the following passage:

> If humanity mobilizes all its wisdom, knowledge, beauty, and especially the all-giving and all-forgiving love and reverence for life, and if a strenuous and sustaining effort of this kind is made by everyone, then the crisis will certainly be ended and a most magnificent new era in human history will be ushered in. It is up to mankind [humankind] to decide what it will do with its future life course.[32]

Throughout history, there have been countless examples of individuals who have set aside their own personal ambitions and interests to devote themselves to the service of others. In the twentieth century, the examples of Mahatma Gandhi, Albert Schweitzer, Mother Theresa, and Martin Luther King, Jr. come quickly to mind in this regard. Each in his or her own way gave up promising careers and personal aspirations in order to dedicate themselves to serving society on a national or international basis. As impressive as these examples are, they should never be allowed to obscure the fact that there

---

32. Pitirim Sorokin, *Modern Historical and Social Philosophies* (New York: Dover Publications, 1963), p. 319 (insert mine).

are many people at every level of society, all walks of life, and in every part of the world, who are working hard to promote the interests of humanity and the world as a whole.

For the cultural personality, altruism is not seen as an alternative to egoism. Rather, both are seen as dual aspects of one reality. While the cultural personality is very much interested in the development of the self, this is not seen as an end in itself, but rather as a means to serving broader interests and the needs of human-kind as a whole. Why is this so essential? It is essential because, as Samuel Butler wisely observed, the works of all people, regardless of whether they are in literature, music, pictures, paintings, architecture, or anything else, are always portraits of the self. And the more people try to conceal it, the more clearly their characters will appear and assert themselves in spite of this.

While altruism is a fundamental characteristic worthy of a great deal of reflection and thought, it is not sufficient in and of itself to ensure that the cultural personality is humane.

It is far from easy to determine how to address this final and most essential characteristic. Perhaps the best place to start is to return to the idea of the harmonious unification of all the characteristics that in totality comprise the cultural personality.

In the process of uniting all these characteristics, the cultural personality is forced to develop many of the sensitivities and sensibilities that are needed to become fully human and truly humane. It is here that the heart, soul, spirit, and senses are fused with the mind and the intellect; egoism is tempered with altruism; beauty, truth, and creativity are brought into line with equality, justice, order, and integrity. The result is an individual who is more settled in the self, as well as more compassionate and respectful of the needs and rights of others.

It is difficult to see how the cultural personality can become truly humane in this sense without plunging deeply into questions of morality. Viewed from this perspective, the current ethical and moral malaise that is sweeping the world must be viewed as a cause for great concern. For in the act of attempting to assert human dominance over nature and making gods of technology and economic growth, are human beings not in danger of losing those moral convictions and ethical ideals that lie at the very heart of all personality development?

Perhaps what is needed most in the world today is the development of a secular moral or ethical code that is capable of assigning to human beings all those fundamental responsibilities that were traditionally associated with God. Of what do these responsibilities consist? Surely they consist of showing compassion and concern for others as well as the sick, the elderly, the poor, and the disadvantaged; lakes, rivers, oceans, and streams; flora and fauna; nature; and other species. Such commitments, especially if they are taken seriously and addressed fully, would compel the cultural personality to develop the sensitivities, sensibilities, and capabilities that are needed to be compassionate in the fullest and most complete sense of the term. For in the process of accepting these responsibilities, the cultural personality would be compelled to develop those deeper and more lasting ethical values, principles, and practices that are needed to become fully committed to the wider cosmic reality and all that is contained in it. This would help to ensure that the cultural personality is not only holistic, centred, authentic, unique, creative, and altruistic, but also humane.

There is no more fitting way to end this chapter than to provide a passage by Prem Kirpal, one of India's most talented and creative individuals and who lived through much of the twentieth century. Not only does the following poem embody many of the qualities and characteristics that combine to comprise the cultural personality, but also it strikes at the heart and soul of what the cultural personality is really all about in fact:

The abiding quality of life-time
Conferred by God on each alive
Is comprised of care of each other,
Quest of love and peace of mind,
Quietness of spirit, and sheer delight
Of being oneself and belonging to all,
Loving and loved in life-time,
Experiencing bliss and ecstasy
With Serenity and Creativity!
May such Quality of Life
Embellish all in time to come
For a great new world of Humanity![33]

---

33. Prem Kirpal, on a personal card sent to the author of this book and printed in India by Kamal Sales Publishers Pty. Ltd.

Chapter Four
The Cultivation of the Cultural Personality

Of all the possible points of penetration into the problem of cultivating the cultural personality, none provides more promise or requires a higher priority than cultivation of the art of seeing.

Cultivation of this art demands a great deal of attention and nurturing because it necessitates the development of a number of interrelated abilities: the ability to see things clearly and as wholes and not just parts of wholes; the ability to detect patterns, themes, and interrelationships between and among the component parts of wholes; the ability to broaden and deepen vision in all directions and view things from the best possible perspective; and the ability to make wise and intelligent decisions about the present and future life course.

Why is it so important for the cultural personality to develop the art of seeing first and foremost? It is important because if we have lost one thing in the modern world, it is the ability to see things clearly and from a holistic rather than partial perspective. Our existing perceptions and perspectives are so fragmented, distorted, specialized, and short-sighted that they lack wisdom, understanding and commonsense. When Fritjof Capra said that all the difficult economic, environmental, social, political, and human problems of our times are really "different facets of one and the same crisis, and that crisis is essentially a crisis of perception,"[34] he put

34. Fritjof Capra, *Uncommon Wisdom: Conversations with Remarkable People* (New York: Simon and Schuster, 1988), p. 232.

his finger on the quintessential importance of the art of seeing as a fundamental prerequisite for effective problem solving.

Ken Wilber was concerned with the same problem in his book *Eye to Eye*. There he talks about developing the three eyes of perception as the key to knowledge and understanding. First, there is the "eye of the flesh." It discloses "the material concrete world of our senses" and therefore the way we "perceive the empirical world of objects in time and space." Second, there is the "eye of reason." It reveals "symbols and images" and consequently the "foundations of the psyche." And third, there is the "eye of contemplation." It is preoccupied with "direct knowledge of spiritual or translogical realities."[35]

Cultivation of the art of seeing was also uppermost in Goethe's mind when he said, "It was with the eye more than with all the other organs that I learned to comprehend the world."[36] He was obviously focusing attention on the critical importance of seeing as a basic necessity for coming to grips with the nature of reality and the self. For how we perceive the world and all that is contained in it as well as how we perceive the self is of crucial importance in determining how we confront problems and decide to live our lives. As a result, it is to the development of the art of seeing that we should direct our attention before anything else if we want to piece together a portrait of how the cultural personality is cultivated in fact.

There is much to be learned about the art of seeing from the artist. Since every work of art is a whole, per-

35. Ken Wilber, *Eye to Eye*, as referenced in R. Ralston, *Teaching the Stones to Speak*. Vision Action Conference, Assembly of B.C. Arts Councils, Kelowna, B. C., 1990.
36. R. King. ed., *Goethe Essays*, p. 236.

spective is of vital importance to the artist and artistic process. And the artist, always conscious of this, is constantly moving around a work of art and stepping back and forth from it in order to see it from the best possible perspective. It is through this process that the artist begins to comprehend the holistic and multifaceted nature of works of art as well as reality, and therefore the need to examine works of art and reality from a variety of perspectives rather than a single perspective. This multidimensional capability is of utmost importance to the cultivation of the art of seeing. For it means that many diverse viewpoints are required if the true nature of works of art and reality are to be revealed.

In the process of constantly moving around a work of art and back and forth from it, the artist reveals something else about the nature of works of art and reality that is of utmost importance to the art of seeing. It is the *interconnected* character of artistic works and reality, and with it, the fact that solutions to problems are not always where they are expected to be. For example, the solution to a problem of too much fullness in a face may lie not in altering the size or shape of the face, but rather in changing the colour of the hair. This is yet another valuable lesson in perspective, since it means that the interconnectedness of problems must always be taken into account if effective solutions to problems are to be found.

There is one other lesson to be learned from the artist in this respect. It has to do with where the viewer positions himself or herself in relation to problems being viewed. Look at a problem from one point of view and it may look like a mountain. Look at it from another, and it may look like a hill. And look at it from still another, and it may disappear entirely. And what is true with respect to the spatial position from which problems are viewed is equally true with respect to the temporal context within which problems are situated. A change in the time horizon within which problems are situated can radically alter their significance. This is yet another valuable lesson in perspective. For it means that where the individual chooses to position himself or herself is of critical importance in determining the nature of problems as well as the real character and essence of reality.

These lessons are extremely important in developing the art of seeing. Regardless of whether it is a painting, a play, a musical composition, or a manuscript, it is not the individual objects, notes, scenes, melodies, words, or chapters that are of greatest importance. Rather, it is the work of art *as a whole*. In effect, every work of art is a holistic entity where the whole takes precedence over the parts. Excesses and imbalances among the parts are permitted, yes, but only in relation to the whole and never for their own sake. And what is true for works of art is also true for people. Every person is an organic whole where the whole does—and should—take precedence over the parts.

If artists have a great deal to contribute to cultivation of the art of seeing, so do scientists. Through their intensive investigations of all manner of things, from the smallest inanimate objects to the largest planetary and galactic systems, scientists have a great deal to contribute to the evolution of this requisite perceptual ability as well. By progressively expanding and intensifying the many different dimensions of seeing, it is possible to view reality in a systematic and disciplined way rather than a spontaneous and random way. The result is a fuller and richer understanding of reality, as well as a deeper and more profound comprehension of the world, nature, the cosmos, and a great deal else.

If there is much to be learned from scientists about the art of seeing, there is also much to be learned from psychologists and psychiatrists. Whereas scientists stretch the dimensions of sight and seeing outward from the smallest and most minute particles to the farthest reaches of the universe, psychologists and psychiatrists push the dimensions of sight and seeing inward into the self. The one is as indispensable as the other. If it is essential to learn more about the nature of reality in an objective sense, it is equally essential to learn more about the nature of the self in a subjective sense. Just as the aim of science is to uncover the true nature of external reality and the universe, so the aim of psychology and psychiatry is to uncover the true nature of internal reality and the self.

If it is the aim of psychologists and psychiatrists to stretch the dimensions of sight and seeing inward into the self, it is the job of historians and futurists to stretch the dimensions of sight and seeing backwards and forwards in time.

Why is it necessary to cultivate the capacity for looking backward into the past and forward into the future? It is necessary in order to broaden and deepen understanding of reality in a much fuller and more comprehensive sense, as well as to comprehend the way the past impacts on and affects the present and the future.

In an historical sense, there is a rich mine to be tapped here. It is essential to plumb the depths of the inexhaustible reservoir of knowledge, wisdom, insight, and understanding inherited from the past. For not only is there an enormous amount to be learned from the past, but it is imperative to avoid the pitfalls of the past, learn from the mistakes of the past, and correct these mistakes in the present and the future.

If the ability to travel backward in historical time is essential in a collective sense, it is also essential in an individual sense. Every individual has a personal history that includes an infinite variety of encounters and events, trials and tribulations, challenges and opportunities, and successes and failures. This vast reservoir of experience is a treasure-trove that should be savoured in good times and bad, but more importantly, is there to be learned from in times of adversity. For it is through this process of assessing and reassessing the past that people learn to confront the realities of the present and take control of their destinies and their lives.

In order to do this fully and effectively, it is necessary to travel forward along the continuum of time and not just back into the past. Whereas the former requires the ability to see and learn from the past, the latter requires the ability to anticipate and prepare properly for the future. The one is as challenging and essential as the other. While it is exceedingly difficult to comprehend the past, particularly in a way that is meaningful, objective, and honest, it is equally difficult to anticipate and prepare properly for the future. Predictions are precarious at the best of times, and much more so when the world is in a state of revolutionary change and dynamic flux.

Nevertheless, it is crucial for people to be as concerned with the future as the past, with the insights of futurists as well as the scholarship of historians. For as John McHale astutely observed, "People survive, uniquely, by their capacity to act in the present on the basis of past experience considered in terms of future consequences."[37]

37. John McHale, *The Future of the Future* (New York: George Braziller, 1969), p. 3.

It is clear from this that the art of seeing should be cultivated by the cultural personality to the point where it acts as a window on the universe as well as on the self. In order to do this effectively, it should be extended as far as possible in all directions: past, present, and future, external and internal, spatial and temporal. Not only should it be finely tuned to the infinite mysteries of the world and the cosmos, but also it should be clearly focused on the most mundane details of daily life. In other words, it should be concerned with the perpetual enlargement of vision, as well as the progressive refinement of vision.

The cultural personality seeks to develop and refine the art of seeing not as an end in itself, but rather as the first step towards the cultivation and refinement of all the other sensory abilities. For what is true with respect to the art of seeing is also true for the art of hearing, touching, smelling, tasting, sensing, and intuiting. Cultivation and refinement of each of these sensorial qualities requires the same kind of continuous care and careful attention that cultivation of the art of seeing necessitates. For aural acuity, tactile sensitivity, olfactory capability, taste discrimination, systematic sensing, and intuitive feeling are equally essential if the object is to expand knowledge and understanding of the external world of reality and the internal world of the self. John Cowper Powys expressed this thought admirably when he said, "the very essence of culture is the conscious development of our awareness of existence."[38]

It is difficult to see how the conscious development of our awareness of existence can be attended to properly and cultivated effectively without a comprehensive education in the arts. For an education in the arts is

38. Powys, *Meaning of Culture*, p. 18.

of quintessential importance in opening up and developing our sensory capabilities and creative faculties to the fullest extent. Through music, there is exposure to sounds, rhythm, harmony, counterpoint, and composition. Through dance, there is exposure to touch, balance, movement, muscle control, and physical co-ordination. Through the visual arts, there is exposure to texture, mass, structure, shape, form, representation, proportion, and the use of colour. And through drama and opera, there is exposure to tragedy, comedy, satire, humour, and pathos. Not only do individuals learn more about the self and the world through an intensive education in the arts, but also they learn to deal creatively and constructively with the countless problems and limitless possibilities that are encountered in life.

One of the most fascinating things about the arts in general and arts education in particular is that the majority of artistic activities can now be enjoyed and experienced through remarkable advances in technology and not just through live performances and exhibitions. Virtually every person in the world can access everything that exists in the arts in both the historical, contemporary, and academic sense today through the miracle of modern technology and communications. They can enjoy the finest popular and classical music, see the most outstanding plays and paintings, walk through the finest museums and galleries, and appreciate all the world's greatest architectural masterpieces through YouTube, iphones, itablets, virtual reality, and many other devices that are owned by family, friends, libraries, schools, community centres, or by people themselves. This is a phenomenal achievement, one that promises to be even more phenomenal in the future.

As our involvement in the arts and arts education intensifies, it becomes apparent that every art form possesses some special quality that makes it distinctive and unique. In music, for example, it is melodies, such as those created by such composers and musicians as Chopin, Schubert, Mendelssohn, Beethoven, the Beatles, and many other melody-makers. This is what gives music its unique significance and universal appeal, which is why some people think music is the highest art form of all.

However, music is not the only art form that possesses a special quality that makes it distinctive and unique. In painting, it is visual representation, as evidenced in the work of painters such as J.M.W. Turner, Vincent van Gogh, Claude Monet, and countless others. In poetry, it is the ability to say profound things with a few simple words, such as when Keats declared, "A thing of beauty is a joy forever," Blake wrote, "To see a world in a grain of sand / And a heaven in a wild flower," and Shakespeare suggested that "All the world's a stage / And all the men and women merely players." Talk about saying profound and powerful things with a few words and therefore with the utmost simplicity!

Then there is dance. What melodies are to music, visual representation is to painting, and simplicity is to poetry, movement is to dance. Here, too, many examples abound, such as Tchaikovsky's *Swan Lake* and *Sleeping Beauty* with their graceful solos and elegant duos set to the most exquisite music imaginable. Architecture also exudes this quality through mass, which is why some people say architecture is "frozen music." This is understandable in view of the fact that some buildings are so graceful, elegant, majestic, and ornate that they really do look like music that has been frozen in time and space, such as the Taj Mahal in Agra, the Blue Mosque in Istanbul, the Jameh Mosque in Isfahan, the Golden Pavilion or Kinkaku-ji in Kyoto, and numerous others.

A particularly important development in arts education was the creation of the Seoul Agenda, which resulted from the Second World Conference on Arts Education convened by UNESCO in Seoul, South Korea in 2010. The most important goals and strategies recognized and established for the Agenda—all of which have a key role to play in the cultivation and development of the cultural personality—are:

- To ensure that arts education is accessible as a fundamental and sustainable component of a high-quality renewal of education;
- To apply arts education principles and practices to contribute to resolving the social and cultural challenges facing today's world;
- To support and enhance the role of arts education in the promotion of social responsibility, social cohesion, cultural diversity, and intercultural dialogue; and
- To affirm arts education as the foundation for balanced creative, cognitive, emotional, aesthetic, and social development of children, youth, and life-long learning.

What education in the arts does for the development of the senses and creative and aesthetic capabilities, education in health and physical fitness does for the development of the body. Without proper training in terms of diet, nutrition, disease prevention, and sufficient exercise of the various parts of the body, the body will not function properly. Regardless of whether it is through calisthenics, Tai Chi, Yoga, a vigorous program of walking, swimming, or some other physical activity designed to relax the muscles and lubricate the joints, the cultural personality is careful to ensure that the body is kept in prime physical condition and good working order.

And this is not all. The cultural personality is equally careful to attend to the cultivation of mental abilities every bit as much as physical, aesthetic, and sensorial abilities. Clearly development of mental abilities requires the ability to cut through the shell of illusion in order to get at the real principles, premises, and assumptions that underlie all things. Far too often, too much attention is paid to superfluous information and outward appearances, thereby leaving too little time to get at the real essence of things. As a result, we often end up dealing with secondary symptoms rather than primary causes.

It is through cultivation of the senses, the body, the mind, and the intellect that the cultural personality begins its ascent into some of the more profound and hidden dimensions of the self. In much the same way as the art of seeing opens the door to all the other senses, so the senses, mind, and body open the doors to the heart, soul, emotions, and spirit.

The development of each of these human faculties is attacked with the same vim, vigour, vitality, and determination as the development of the senses, the body, the mind, and the intellect. The goal is always self-improvement or "self-actualization," to use Maslow's evocative phrase.

Considerable care should be taken to ensure that the idea of self-improvement is not confused with the idea of perfectibility. For the cultural personality, perfectibility is something worth striving for, but is ultimately unattainable. In the first place, it demands perfect knowledge and understanding, which, as we have seen, stands well beyond the capabilities and potentialities of the cultural personality. For regardless of how much the cultural personality sees, senses, feels, learns, and knows, it is always possible to see, sense, feel, learn, and know much more. This is why "the whole" is always viewed in dynamic rather than static terms, as an open agenda rather than a closed system. Moreover, the cultural personality is always aware of its own *imperfectability*. While perfectibility is a goal worthy of pursuit, the cultural personality is always conscious of the inherent limitations and shortcomings which stand in the way of ever achieving this in fact.

It is through recognition of the necessity and inevitability of imperfectability that the cultural personality slowly but surely develops the sense of humility, awe, wonder, and appreciation that forms the basis of cosmic consciousness. Clearly, this cosmic capability lies at the very core of the cultural personality. It is external in the sense that it radiates outward in order to embrace the ever-expanding dimensions of the world and the universe. It is internal in the sense that it penetrates deeply into the psyche in order to embrace all that it is possible to know and understand about the self. As a result, it stretches as far as possible in both directions, even though it is never possible to know what exists at the outer edges of the universe or the inner limits of the self.

Some contend that cosmic consciousness is such a rarefied affair that it can only be experienced by a few very select and fortunate individuals. In his book *Cosmic*

Consciousness: A Study in the Evolution of the Human Mind, the medical doctor, Richard Maurice Bucke, identifies three types of consciousness: *simple consciousness,* or awareness of one's bodily organs as well as the things that go on around one; *self-consciousness,* or awareness not only of one's bodily organs and the immediate external environment but also awareness of oneself as a distinct entity apart from the rest of the universe; and *cosmic consciousness,* or awareness of the cosmos as an "ordered whole."[39] Having set out these three different types of consciousness, Bucke then goes on to describe cosmic consciousness in much more detail:

> Along with the consciousness of the cosmos there occurs an intellectual enlightenment of *illumination* which alone would place the individual on a new plane of existence—would make him [her] almost a member of a new species. To this is added a state of moral exaltation, an indescribable feeling of elevation, elation, and joyousness, and a quickening of the moral sense, which is fully as striking and more important both to the individual and to the race than is the enhanced intellectual power. With these come what may be called a sense of immortality, a consciousness of eternal life, not a conviction that he [she] shall have this, but the consciousness that he [she] has it already.[40]

Using the third rather than first person pronoun, Bucke then goes on to describe the intensity of his own experience with cosmic consciousness and this remarkable phenomenon:

39. Richard Maurice Bucke, *Cosmic Consciousness: A Study in the Evolution of the Human Mind* (New York: E.P. Dutton, 1969), pp. 1–2 (inserts mine).
40. Ibid., p. 3.

His mind ... was calm and peaceful. He was in a state of quiet, almost passive enjoyment. All at once, without warning of any kind, he found himself wrapped around as it were by a flame-coloured cloud. For an instant he thought of fire, some sudden conflagration in the great city; the next, he knew that the light was within himself. Directly afterwards came upon him a sense of exultation, of immense joyousness accompanied or immediately followed by an intellectual illumination quite impossible to describe. Into his brain streamed one momentary lightning-flash of the Brahmic Splendor which has ever since lightened his life; upon his heart fell one drop of Brahmic Bliss, leaving thenceforward for always an aftertaste of heaven. Among other things he did not come to believe, he saw and knew that the Cosmos is not dead matter but a living Presence, that the soul of man [woman] is immortal, that the universe is so built and ordered that without any peradventure all things work together for the good of each and all, that the foundation principle of the world is what we call love and that the happiness of every one is in the long run absolutely certain. He claims that he learned more within the few seconds during which the illumination lasted than in previous months or even years of study, and that he learned much that no study could ever have taught.[41]

According to Bucke, eventually humanity *as a species* may well be able to realize this utopian state of affairs, even though it is limited to a very few select individuals at present. Whether or not this ethereal state of affairs may ever be actually attainable, are there not grounds for asking if the experience of cosmic consciousness is not much more common than is generally realized? While cosmic consciousness may be a highly rarified and personal affair that defies scientific confirmation

41. Ibid., pp. 9–10 (insert mine).

or interpersonal comparison, who has not experienced the feeling of Brahmic splendour or bliss that Bucke describes at one time or another in their lives, when the sense of ecstasy and serenity that comes from some unique experience with other people, the arts, sciences, nature, or the natural environment is so profound and intense that for the flash of a second there is a feeling of immortality and the entire universe and all of humanity seem united as in a unitary and ordered whole? Surely cosmic consciousness is more commonplace than some people may be willing to admit.

Possibly it was cosmic consciousness that Herman Hesse had in mind when he wrote the following passage in *The Glass Bead Game*:

> World history is a race with time, a scramble for profit, for power, for treasures. What counts is who has the strength, luck, or vulgarity not to miss the opportunity. The achievements of thought, of culture, of the arts are just the opposite. They are always an escape from the serfdom of time, man [woman] crawling out of the muck of his [her] instinct and out of his [her] sluggishness and climbing to a higher plane, to timelessness, liberation from time, divinity.[42]

In the process of striving to achieve this desirable state of affairs, the cultural personality comes face to face with the holistic nature of the universe and of life. When Goethe said, "Who wills the highest, must will the whole," he put his finger on the crux of this matter. For in the process of willing the highest, the cultural personality not only comes face to face with the holistic nature of the universe and life, but also with the means of uniting all the various human faculties and capabili-

42. Herman Hesse, *The Glass Bead Game* (New York: Bantam Books, 1977), p. 55 (inserts mine).

ties in a symbiotic and unitary relationship. The senses, body, mind, intellect, heart, soul, and spirit become one, so to speak, indispensable elements in the overall make-up of the individual person. Surely this is what Jan Christiaan Smuts had in mind when he made the following observation:

> The great practical problem before the Personality is thus to effectuate and preserve its wholeness through the harmonizing of its several activities, and the prevention among them of any random discord or sedition, whereby one or other might be enabled to assume ascendancy over the rest and so prepare the way for the disintegration and destruction of the whole....
>
> In proportion as a personality really becomes such, it acquires more of the character of wholeness; body and mind, intellect and heart, will and emotions, while not separately repressed but on the contrary fostered and developed, are yet all collectively harmonized and blended into one integral whole; the character becomes more massive, the entire man [woman] becomes more of a piece; and the will or conscious rational direction, which is not a separate agency hostile to these individual factors, but the very root and expression of their joint and harmonious action, becomes more silently and smoothly powerful; the wear and tear of internal struggle disappears; the friction and waste which accompany the warfare in the soul are replaced by peace and unity and strength; till at last Personality stands forth in its ideal purity, integrity and wholeness.[43]

It is difficult to see how the cultural personality can stand forth in all "its ideal purity, integrity, and wholeness" without developing a comprehensive, compassionate, and enlightened *cultural* worldview. This worldview

43. Smuts, *Holism*, pp. 296, 298 (insert mine).

is very different than the economic worldview, the political worldview, the technological worldview, and all other worldviews that see the world in terms of its parts rather than as a whole.

In the process of developing a worldview of this type, the cultural personality learns to take a consuming interest in all things. To do so effectively requires exploration of everything: large and small; esoteric and commonplace; popular and elite. Nothing is rejected, ignored, or taken for granted since everything that is germane to culture, the human condition, the world, and the cosmos is examined in depth and with great interest. Whether it is the arts, the sciences, religion, politics, philosophy, economics, social affairs, technology, or the environment, all fields of knowledge and all disciplines are actively and openly explored because they contain indispensable clues to the effective formulation and implementation of this cultural way of looking at the world, life, people, all the diverse cultures and civilizations of the world, the natural environment, other species, and the universe as a whole, This is because culture lies at the root and is the centerpiece of all these various entities and activities in the world when it is perceived and understood in holistic rather than partial terms.

Cultivation of this cultural worldview will require the development of educational and learning processes and possibilities that are different than those in existence today. Whereas most contemporary educational and learning processes and possibilities are focused on the mastery of a single discipline and acquisition of a narrow range of specialized skills and abilities, the educational and learning processes advocated here are predicated on exploration and discovery of many disciplines, as well as acquisition of a very diversified set of skills and abilities. Not only is this more in keeping with the true nature of the cultural personality, but also it is more in tune with the newly emerging global reality.

Development of this significantly broader approach to education and learning will be no easy matter. All people are products of their society to the point where they take many aspects of it for granted and accept them without reservation or qualification. To develop an educational and learning system that is finely tuned to the realities of the present and requirements of the future does not mean rejecting those aspects of one's own society that are taken for granted. Rather, it means critically examining every aspect in order to determine what is relevant and what is irrelevant. One of the best ways to do this is to juxtapose and compare one's own society with that of others. For intersocietal comparison and analysis is one of the best ways of all of exposing the strengths and shortcomings of one's own society, as well as those aspects of one's society that are most pertinent to the human condition and world situation.

However difficult it is to stand outside one's own society in order to evaluate it with an objective and critical eye, it is even more difficult to stand outside the self in order to see it in a detached and objective manner.

If only we could see ourselves as others see us! If so, we would be able to deal with our problems, possibilities, and lives far more effectively. Things that are patently obvious to others are often clouded and obscured to the self. To see ourselves as others see us—our strengths and shortcomings, insecurities and instabilities, problems, potential, and opportunities—would be to take a giant leap forward in developing a fuller and more complete understanding of the self. Perhaps this is why the cultural personality is always engaged in actively searching out the opinions of others, as well as using other people as a mirror to see the self. For as difficult as the art of self-assessment is, it is of quintessential importance to the effective cultivation of the cultural personality.

It is through the ability to see oneself as others see it, as well as to evaluate oneself with a discriminating and discerning eye, that the cultural personality comes face to face with its real essence. What is it in the final analysis that gives the cultural personality its real essence, meaning, and identity? In the end, it is the sense of fulfilment that comes from taking the time and trouble to develop an overall way of life that is consistent with the nature of reality and the self as well as the dictates of the natural environment, the world, and the cosmos. By its very nature, this way of life is indigenous rather than imitative. Not only is it hammered out on the anvil of life's experiences, but also it is highly original and authentic in every conceivable way. In effect, it is fashioned not by allowing others to dictate what is important or how to live our lives, but rather by deciding for oneself what is important and how we want to live our lives and accept responsibility for this.

In the process of hammering out this total or all-encompassing way of life and accepting full responsibility for it, the cultural personality recognizes that it has mastered not only the art of seeing and all other sensorial and non-sensorial qualities and abilities, but more importantly, the art of being. The reason for this is readily apparent and crystal clear. In the act of dealing with all the trials and tribulations that manifest themselves in the external world of reality and internal world of self, the cultural personality is compelled to cultivate those capabilities, sensitivities, and sensibilities that are imperative to live life as an ordered, comprehensive, coherent, and harmonious whole.

Chapter V
The Conduct of the Cultural Personality

If it is necessary to come to grips with the cultivation of the cultural personality, it is also necessary to come to grips with the conduct of the cultural personality. Whereas the former is concerned largely with education and the realm of thoughts and ideas, the latter is concerned primarily with practice and the realm of action and reality. While the one is equally as essential as the other, in the end it will be through deeds and actions more than thoughts and ideas that the cultural personality will make its mark on the world.

In order for the cultural personality to take its rightful place alongside other personality types as a guide to human behaviour, it will have to provide a powerful example for others to follow. Such an example will have to evolve from the highest ideals of human conduct, as well as inspire the noblest forms of human action.

Providing exemplary conduct in the age we are living in at present will be no easy task. In fact, it will probably be the most difficult task of all, given the fact that the temptations of living in a materialistic, secular, and technologically-dominated age are so great that exemplary conduct and action may be confined to people who are the most courageous and committed.

Strong ethical leadership is the key to achieving this task. It grows out of the realization that ethical values have the greatest importance for our lives as well as for communities, societies, and countries, and therefore demands our highest priority and attention. Albert Schweitzer explains why this is so necessary:

We may take as the essential element in civilization the ethical perfecting of the individual and of society as well. But at the same time, every spiritual and every material step in advance has a significance for civilization. The will to civilization is then the universal will to progress which is conscious of the ethical as the highest value for all. In spite of the great importance we attach to the triumphs of knowledge and achievement, it is nevertheless obvious that only a humanity which is striving after ethical ends can in full measure share in the blessings brought by material progress and become master of the dangers which accompany it. To the generation which had adopted a belief in an immanent power of progress realizing itself, in some measure, naturally and automatically, and which thought that it no longer needed any ethical ideals but could advance to its goal by means of knowledge and achievement alone, terrible proof was being given by its present position of the error into which it had sunk.... But what is the nature of the attitude toward life in which the will to general progress and to ethical progress are alike founded and in which they are bound together? It consists in an ethical affirmation of the world and of life.[44]

For the cultural personality, human conduct is first and foremost an ethical affair and responsibility. It involves not only recognition of the ethical foundations of human existence in general and human behaviour in particular, but also acceptance of the fact there are ethical implications and consequences to everything we do, regardless of whether it is confronting the self, dealing with others, making consumer choices, participating in political causes, or interacting with the natural environment and other species.

Commitment to the existential conviction that in

44. Albert Schweitzer, *Out of My Life and Thought: An Autobiography* (New York: Holt, Rinehart and Winston, 1964), pp. 149–150.

committing ourselves we are committing the whole of humanity would seem to provide a logical point of departure for this.

Adherence to this conviction requires the cultural personality to think long and hard about the ethical consequences of behaviour. This necessitates a kind of "reverential thinking," a willingness to consider the impact of behaviour not only on the self, but also on other human beings, other forms of plant, animal, and mineral life, and ultimately, the cosmos as a whole. Reverential thinking of this type compels the cultural personality to probe deeply into matters of the heart, soul, and spirit in order to evolve modes of behaviour that do as little damage as possible to everything that exists outside the self.

For the cultural personality, reverential thinking is not an end in itself, but rather the first step towards reverential action. If consumption practices are deemed to be disrespectful of the natural environment or wasteful of resources, they are not condoned regardless of how much they satisfy personal needs and preferences. If success means running roughshod over the needs, rights, and privileges of others, it is not pursued regardless of how much it might advance individual interests. If standards of living in one part of the world are enjoyed at the expense of people living in other parts of the world, they are not condoned regardless of how fulfilling they might be or actually are.

In each of these cases, and others too numerous to enumerate here, the cultural personality is careful to choose a course of action that does not involve exploiting others or the natural environment in order to satisfy the needs and interests of the self.

Albert Schweitzer was one of the greatest advocates

of reverential action. To him, all life was precious, and therefore had to be protected at all costs. Let us quote again from this remarkable individual, since he has much to say that is relevant to the conduct of the cultural personality.

> Ethics is nothing else than reverence for life. Reverence for life affords me my fundamental principle of morality, namely, that good consists in maintaining, assisting and enhancing life, and that to destroy, to harm or to hinder life is evil....
>
> A man [woman] is really ethical only when he [she] obeys the constraint laid on him [her] to help all life which he [she] is able to succor, and when he [she] goes out of his [her] way to avoid injuring anything living. He [she] does not ask how far this or that life deserves sympathy as valuable in itself, nor how far it is capable of feeling. To him [her] life as such is sacred. He [she] shatters no ice crystal that sparkles in the sun, tears no leaf from its tree, breaks off no flower, and is careful not to crush any insect as he [she] walks.[45]

It would be foolish to contend that the cultural personality can always be a tower of ethical strength or moral perfection in this sense. What the cultural personality is always striving to do, however, is live a way of life that is based on fulfilling personal aspirations without usurping the needs, rights, and requirements of others. If this cannot be achieved with one mode of behaviour, as indicated earlier, the cultural personality sets in motion other modes of behaviour and action that are capable of achieving this.

In attempting to glean a clearer impression and understanding of the ethical ideals which lie at the heart

45. Joy, ed., *Schweitzer: An Anthology*, pp. 259–260 and p. 273 (inserts mine).

of the cultural personality, it may be helpful to examine the two Chinese notions of "face." The first is *mien-tzu*; and the second is *lien*. This is how Hu Hsien-Chin elaborates on these two notions. Their relevance for the cultural personality is immediately apparent:

> [M]ien-tzu ... is a reputation achieved through getting on in life, through success and ostentation. This is prestige that is accumulated by means of personal effort or clever maneuvering. For this kind of recognition ego is dependent at all times on the external environment. The other kind of "face," lien ... is the respect of the group for a man [woman] with a good moral reputation: the man [woman] who will fulfil his [her] obligations regardless of the hardships involved, who under all circumstances shows himself [herself] a decent human being. It represents the confidence of society in the integrity of ego's moral character, the loss of which makes it impossible for him [her] to function properly within the community. Lien is both a social sanction for enforcing moral standards and an internalized sanction.[46]

While the cultural personality is obviously an admixture of both these characteristics, it is clear where the real emphasis lies. It lies with *lien*. While the cultural personality is concerned with personal success and fulfilment as much as anyone else, this is not achieved at the expense of others. Whatever can be accomplished by maintaining ethical integrity is accomplished; whatever cannot be accomplished by maintaining these ideals is discarded or rejected.

It is out of commitment to ethical ideals, rather than slavish adherence to the norms and mores of a partic-

46. Douglas Haring, ed., *Personal Character and Cultural Milieu* (Syracuse, NY: Syracuse University Press. 1964), p. 447 (inserts mine).

ular community, society, or culture, that the cultural personality seeks to fashion its conduct in the world. The goal is always working out for oneself the type of conduct and behavior that is most appropriate under the circumstances, not following some predetermined course of action or prescribed set of rules.

Commitment to this goal causes the cultural personality to transcend the limitations and shortcomings of cultures when it is necessary. This makes the cultural personality a "culture-maker" rather than "culture-taker," since the norms, ideological beliefs, and systems that underlie a culture are constantly being analyzed and assessed. Edward Hall explains why this is so necessary:

> One cannot normally transcend one's culture without first exposing its major hidden axioms and unstated assumptions concerning what life is all about—how it is lived, viewed, analyzed, talked about, described, and changed. Because cultures are wholes, are systematic (composed of interrelated systems in which each aspect is functionally interrelated with all other parts), and are highly contexted as well, it is hard to describe them from the outside. A given culture cannot be understood simply in terms of context or parts. One has to know how the whole system is put together, how the major systems and dynamisms function, and how they are interrelated.[47]

Whenever the norms, ideological beliefs, and systems of a culture are based on faulty or implicit assumptions, or they conflict with the interests of the culture as a whole, the cultural personality is anxious to contest, challenge, and change them. Whether or not it is pos-

47. Edward Hall, *Beyond Culture* (Garden City, NY: Anchor Press/Doubleday, 1976), p. 195.

sible to do this depends on a variety of factors. For as Goethe said in a letter to Schiller: "Your own epoch you cannot change. You can, however, oppose its trends and lay the groundwork for auspicious developments."[48]

In the process of laying the groundwork for auspicious developments, the cultural personality is compelled to become "cause oriented." Rather than calculating everything on the basis of how it advances personal interests or career aspirations, the cultural personality evaluates everything in terms of how it advances specific causes. If something doesn't advance a cause to which the cultural personality is committed, it is not pursued regardless of how it satisfies personal objectives or career ambitions.

And what are these causes to which the cultural personality is deeply and irrefutably committed? In one form or another, they are causes that are concerned with environmental sustainability, resource conservation, freedom, liberty, human dignity, and equality regardless of social status, religious persuasion, economic circumstances, gender, geographical location, or any other factor.

A seminal step was taken in the right direction in this regard when the Universal Declaration of Human Rights was signed by the General Assembly of the United Nations in 1948. Included among the many articles aimed at recognizing and ensuring the rights of every person in the world were two articles designed to protect the cultural rights of the individual and increase citizen participation in cultural life:

Article 22
Everyone, as a member of society, has the right to social security and is entitled to realization, through national

48. R. King, ed., *Goethe Essays*, p. ix.

effort and international co-operation and in accordance with the organization and resources of each State, of the economic, social and cultural rights indispensable for his [her] dignity and the free development of his [her] personality.

Article 27
Everyone has the right to participate in the cultural life of the community, to enjoy the arts and to share in scientific advancement and its benefits.

Everyone has the right to the protection of the moral and material interests resulting from any scientific, literary or artistic production of which he [she] is the author.[49]

Following the signing of the Declaration of Human Rights by the United Nations in 1948, the entire world became preoccupied with the realization of human rights in general and people's individual rights in particular. This was understandable and necessary. The Second World War had just ended and millions of people in many parts of the world had lost any rights they may have had during the war and for a long time thereafter. As a result, great advances were made—and have been made since that time—in many if not all parts of the world due to the articulation and enforcement of the Declaration. This has been a remarkable achievement and a real success, even if there is still an enormous amount of work to be done in this area.

Unfortunately, however, preoccupation with people's rights has obscured and neglected the fact that people have responsibilities as well as rights. This has become very evident in the modern world, as has the

49. UNESCO, *Cultural Rights as Human Rights* (Paris: UNESCO, 1970), pp. 117–122 (inserts mine).

fact that humanity is now paying a severe price for not recognizing the responsibilities people have as members of groups, communities, and societies as well as citizens of countries. Not only do they have rights to enjoy, but also they have responsibilities to execute in return if groups, communities, societies, countries, and the world as a whole are to function effectively.

In recent years, this has highlighted the need to create a Universal Declaration of Human Rights and Responsibilities. Of what do these responsibilities consist? Surely they consist, among countless other things, of: conservation of nature, the natural environment, other species, and global eco-systems; decreasing demands made on the world's scarce resources; acting in a cooperative and conciliatory rather than aggressive and confrontational manner; learning about culture and all the diverse cultures and civilizations of the world; pursuing peace, harmony, and unity rather than war, conflict, and violence; preventing terrorism and terrorist attacks; dealing with diversity and cultural differences effectively; maintaining a high level of health care and physical fitness; being a responsible citizen; helping others; appreciating the values, ways of life, and worldviews of other people; assisting the needy and the unfortunate; and sharing income and wealth more fairly and fully. In order to achieve this, it is necessary to take a cultural or holistic approach to citizenship and therefore to be concerned with the other and not just the self, giving as well as taking, and treating people with dignity, reverence, and respect.

It is through commitment to responsibilities such as these, as well as making it possible for all people to become full and active participants in communities and countries, that the cultural personality seeks to have an impact on the world. This involves fighting for justice and equality in all their diverse forms and manifestations. Whereas socialists view this fight largely in terms of economic, social, and political justice and equality, the cultural personality views this fight primarily in terms of justice and equality in all aspects of life. For socialists, the challenge is to eliminate all forms of economic, social, and political exploitation and discrimination. For the cultural personality, the challenge is to eliminate all forms of exploitation and discrimination clear and simple: not only in economic, social, and political terms, but also in institutional, bureaucratic, legal, environmental, and all other forms that rob people of their creativity, achievements, dignity, freedom, or integrity.

In the process of fighting to combat all forms of exploitation, the cultural personality slowly but surely strengthens commitment to the higher ideals of culture and of life. Here again, Schweitzer has something very powerful and pertitent to say:

> The ripeness that our development must aim at is one which makes us simpler, more truthful, purer, more peace loving, meeker, kinder, more sympathetic. That is the only way in which we are to sober down with age. That is the process in which the soft iron of youthful idealism hardens into the steel of a full-grown idealism which can never be lost.[50]

Pitirim Sorokin was equally aware of the importance of these ideals, and the need to ensure that they are situated properly in a much broader and deeper cultural and cosmic context. Speaking of the need for a heightened sense of human consciousness, he said:

---

50. Joy, ed., *Schweitzer: An Anthology*, p. 131.

The most urgent need of our time is the man [woman] who can control himself [herself] and his [her] lusts, who is compassionate to all his [her] fellow men [women], who can see and seek for the eternal values of culture and society, and who deeply feels his [her] unique responsibility to the universe.[51]

Foremost among this commitment to "see and seek for the eternal values of culture and society" is commitment to respect and disseminate the tangible and intangible cultural heritage of humankind. The more the cultural personality transcends the limits of individual cultures, the more it gains understanding of the vast reservoir of inherited knowledge, wisdom, artefacts, insights, and ideas that constitute the universal legacy of history. In much the same way that it is anxious to gain access to this indispensable treasure-trove in order to educate, enlighten, and improve the self, so it is equally anxious to share this precious gift with each and every member of the human family.

It is here that the cultural personality parts company with cultural purists and imperialists. Whereas the latter are concerned with asserting the superiority of one culture over another, largely for the purpose of imposing the values and objectives of one culture on another culture or on many cultures, the former is concerned with sharing the fruits of all the diverse cultures in the world with the whole of humanity. In other words, the cultural personality is concerned with those acts of generosity and benevolence that promote real trust, reciprocity, and sharing in the world. The great Indian poet and sage, Rabindranath Tagore, foresaw this day when he said, "We must prepare the field for the co-operation

---

51. Pitirim Sorokin, *Social and Cultural Dynamics* (Boston: Sargent Publisher,1957), p. 628 (inserts mine).

of all the cultures of the world where all will give and take from each other. This is the keynote of the coming age."[52] Mahatma Gandhi reinforced this idea when he said, "I do not want my house to be walled in on all sides and my windows to be stuffed. I want the culture of all the lands to be blown about my house as freely as possible. But I refuse to be blown off my feet by any."[53]

In the final analysis, it is through co-operation and sharing, rather than competition and hoarding, that the cultural personality seeks to make its mark on the world. The object is always to create the conditions for a better world—a world characterized by more dignity, justice, equality, peace, harmony, and freedom for the whole of humanity. Such a world requires a continuous outpouring of those qualities that are most deeply entrenched in the cultural personality: compassion, caring, sharing, concern for others, and most of all, human love and affection.

There is one final matter that must be addressed here. It is the *positioning* of the cultural personality in the world. For, as we observed earlier, where the individual positions himself or herself in the world is of vital importance in determining the ultimate outcome of developments and events. Presumably this is what Kant had in mind when he said:

> If there is any science [humanity] really needs, it is the one I teach, of how to occupy properly that place in creation that is assigned to [it], and how to learn from it what one must learn in order to be a man [woman].[54]

52. Quoted in D. Paul Schafer, *Canada's International Cultural Relations* (Ottawa: Department of External Affairs, 1979), p. 2.
53. Quoted in *Our Creative Diversity: Report of the World Commission on Culture and Development* (Paris: UNESCO, 1995), p.73.
54. Quoted in E. Becker, *The Denial of Death* (London: The Free Press, 1972), p. 255 (inserts mine).

There is much to be learned about the problem of positioning from people like Gandhi and Mother Theresa, as well as from many other leaders who have had a profound impact on the world. Whether Gandhi and Mother Theresa set out to change the world is impossible to say. What is possible to say, however, is the fact that they had an incredible impact on the world and course of history by deliberately positioning themselves in a very specific part of the world working with local people. They did not go tearing around the world attempting to improve conditions for all people. Rather, they stayed largely where they were, allowing the force of their personalities and the passion of their convictions to speak for them.

Much may be learned from these two individuals that is germane to the conduct of the cultural personality. Rather than setting out to influence the course of world events, the cultural personality is constantly striving to put into practice in everyday life those ethical, spiritual, and human qualities that are needed to inspire others and produce practical results. The focus is not so much on "thinking globally but acting locally," although this is very much a part of it. Rather it is on "thinking cosmically, but acting personally." To do this is to allow the individual person to discover within the self the "reflection of the cosmos and its supreme unifying principle."[55] Surely this is what Goethe had in mind when he said, "live in the whole, in the good, in the beautiful." It is also what Joseph Campbell had in mind when he said, "follow your bliss." For the cultural personality, this is what life and living are really all about.

55. Symposium on Science and Culture for the 21st Century: Agenda for Survival, "Survival in the 21st Century: The Vancouver Declaration," *IFDA Dossier* 77 (May/June. 1990), pp. 47–50.

Selected Readings

Gordon Allport, *Pattern and Growth in Personality* (New York: Holt, Rinehart and Winston, 1987).

Matthew Arnold, *Culture and Anarchy* (Cambridge: Cambridge University Press, 1955).

Ruth Benedict, *Patterns of Culture* (New York: Penguin Books, 1946).

David Bohm and F. David Peat, *Science, Order and Creativity* (New York: Bantam Books, 1987).

A.A. Brill, ed. *The Basic Writings of Sigmund Freud* (New York: Modern Library, New York, 1938).

Richard Bucke, *Cosmic Consciousness: A Study of the Evolution of the Human Mind.* (New York: E.P. Dutton, 1969).

Fritjof Capra, *Uncommon Wisdom: Conversations with Remarkable People* (New York: Simon and Schuster,1988).

James Feibleman, *The Theory of Human Culture* (New York: Humanities Press, 1968).

Josef Goldbrunner, *Individualism: A Study of the Depth Psychology of Carl Gustav Jung* (Notre Dame, IN: University of Notre Dame Press, 1966).

Douglas Haring, ed. *Personal Character and Cultural Milieu* (Syracuse: University Press, 1949).

Melville Herskovits, *Cultural Relativism: Perspectives in Cultural Pluralism* (New York: Random House, 1972).

Melville Herskovits, *Man and His Works* (New York: Alfred A. Knopf, 1964).

John Honigman, *Culture and Personality* (New York: Harper and Row Publishers,1954).

Francis Hsu, ed. *Aspects of Culture and Personality* (New York: Abelard-Schuman, 1954).

Charles R. Joy, ed. *Albert Schweitzer: An Anthology* (Boston: The Beacon Press, 1959).

Carl Gustav Jung, *Modern Man in Search of a Soul* (New York: Harcourt, Brace and World, 1933).

C. Kluckhohn, H.A. Murray, and D.M. Schneider, eds. *Personality in Nature, Society and Culture* (New York: Alfred A. Knopf, 1953).

Ralph Linton, *The Study of Man* (New York: Appleton-Century-Crofts, Inc., 1936).

Ralph Linton, *The Cultural Background of Personality* (New York: Appleton-Century-Crofts, Inc., 1945).

Abraham H. Maslow, *Motivation and Personality* (New York: Harper and Row Publishers, 1970).

John Powys, *The Meaning of Culture* (New York: W.W. Norton and Company Inc. 1929).

Stansfield Sargent and Marian Smith, *Culture and Personality* ((New York: Viking Fund, 1949).

P.A. Sorokin, *Explorations in Altruistic Love and Behaviour* (Boston: Beacon Press, 1950).

Jan Christiaan Smuts, *Holism and Evolution* (New York: The Viking Press, 1961).

Anthony Wallace, *Culture and Personality* (New York: Random House, 1967).